Glimmerings II

Glimmerings
II

Another 1001 Thoughts, Ideas,
Observations, Musings
Reflections, and Comments
On Whatever Comes to Mind

Robert A. Harris

.:Virtual**Salt**
Publishing
Tustin

Glimmerings II
Another 1001 Thoughts, Ideas, Observations, Musings, Reflections, and Comments On Whatever Comes to Mind

ISBN 978-1-941233-09-2

VirtualSalt® Publishing
Tustin, California

www.virtualsalt.com

I have one word to say upon the subject of profound writers, *who are grown very numerous of late; and, I know very well, the judicious world is resolved to list me in that number. I conceive therefore, as to the business of being* profound, *that it is with* writers, *as with* wells; *a person with good eyes may see to the bottom of the deepest, provided any* water *be there; and, that often, when there is nothing in the world at the bottom, besides* dryness *and* dirt, *tho' it be but a yard and half under ground, it shall pass, however, for wondrous* deep, *upon no wiser a reason than because it is wondrous* dark.

— *Jonathan Swift*, A Tale of a Tub

Words are like leaves; and where they most abound,
Much fruit of sense beneath is rarely found.
. . . .
But true expression, like th' unchanging sun,
Clears, and improves whate'er it shines upon.

— *Alexander Pope*, An Essay on Criticism

The mind is but a barren soil; a soil which is soon exhausted, and will produce no crop, or only one, unless it be continually fertilized and enriched with foreign matter.

— *Joshua Reynolds*, Discourses on Art

The greatest part of a writer's time is spent in reading, in order to write; a man will turn over half a library to make one book.

— *Samuel Johnson, quoted in Boswell's* Life of Johnson

Samuel Johnson, *Rambler No. 2*

Perhaps no class of the human species requires more to be cautioned against this anticipation of happiness, than those that aspire to the name of authors.

There is nothing more dreadful to an author than neglect, compared with which reproach, hatred, and opposition, are names of happiness; yet this worst, this meanest fate, every man who dares to write has reason to fear.

It may not be unfit for him who makes a new entrance into the lettered world, so far to suspect his own powers as to believe that he possibly may deserve neglect. . . . For this suspicion, every catalogue of a library will furnish sufficient reason; as he will find it crowded with names of men, who, though now forgotten, were once no less enterprising or confident than himself. . . .

Introduction

Glimmerings II is a second collection of thoughts and observations from my personal notebook, this portion spanning the thirty-two years from 1982 to 2014, from my age 31 to 63. It appears that the busyness of life has caused my glimmering to slow down, since readers of *Glimmerings I* will recall that the first 1001 were written in only eight years.

Nevertheless, there should appear somewhat more maturity in this volume, with, I hope, at least as much food for thought, entertainment, and enjoyment as in the first volume. Having just read over the collection again in preparing this volume, I do realize much more starkly that I am not a politically correct thinker. However, I would remind the reader that a main purpose for reading philosophy (or these thoughts, if the reader cannot grant them the label of philosophy) is not to accumulate right answers (though that is another purpose at times), but to find food for thought, interesting questions, or even provocation. If the reader deems me wrong, foolish, naïve, out of touch, biased, Neanderthal or whatever other adjective suits, I hope I am so in an interesting way that will produce thought and increased clarity. I've often said that Plato is wrong in very interesting ways, and for that reason alone deserves our attention.

I have no objection to the reader's flinging this volume across the room in a fit of disgust (though e-readers should restrain themselves), as long as the book provokes further thought. And, of course, I hope the book, however bloodied from repeated body slams, will be picked up again and again, if for no other reason than to discover what additional outrage can be found in it.

The narrator in Jonathan Swift's satire *A Tale of a Tub* threatens his readers with additional works, including one wherein he writes on nothing. This makes me cautious of saying that there might be a third 1001 Glimmerings, but the fact is I am still collecting my thoughts (double entendre intentional) and noting them down. I am now in a position where I can read more than I have been able to do in recent years, and reading is a great — perhaps the greatest — stimulus to ideas for me. So, if you read just two of these Glimmerings a day, one in the morning and one in the evening, by the time you finish the book, there just might be a third volume for your enjoyment or exasperation.

At any rate, I hope you find here what you came to find, and that your reading will be rewarded.

.

Tustin, California
March, 2014

Glimmerings II

1002. When an "if only" is granted, it is usually followed by a "but I thought—."

1003. Beware of the man who squints while denying the existence of light.

1004. He used to think there was nothing more to be desired in life than the bottles of his wine cellar. Then one day he stepped on a nail and became a philosopher.

1005. "He is not saying what everyone else is saying; therefore, let us stone him." Why is this such a popular doctrine? "He is saying something new and different from everyone else; therefore, let us follow him into the quicksand." Why is this such a popular doctrine?

1006. "Truth, wisdom, morality, philosophy—yes these are all worthy and great things. But after all, thinking is hard work and I'm just an ordinary man; so I'll just sit back and scratch my belly while someone else figures it all out."

1007. We need to alter our attitudes toward each other from "Mistakes will not be tolerated" to "Mistakes are welcome." We are humans and humans *do* make mistakes, and, I hope, they learn and grow as a result. Life is a panorama of error and failure. By declaring that we will not tolerate the inevitable, we make life anxious, frustrating, and unhappy. We make each other so afraid to fail or to reveal our imperfections that all ambition and risk-taking are (as Johnson might say) refrigerated.

Children and spouses should be allowed to say and do

"foolish" things. Don't get upset about it. That's how we all learn, how we discover what we really think, how we find out who we are. And besides, today's foolishness sometimes turns out to have been very wise. We see only in part, and often each of us sees a different part.

Reason cannot, and should not, always win. Many emotional and psychological needs and satisfactions are largely if not totally irrational. But they are very real, nonetheless.

1008. Take a lesson, O wise man, from a four-year-old child: when he falls, he gets right back up.

1009. **Real Life #1**.

"There's Tom. Isn't he just great? So good looking. Ooh, I think I'm in love. What do you think?"

"I don't know. He *is* really handsome, but—"

"But what?"

"Well, he—he doesn't—he doesn't have, you know, *dandruff.*"

"So?"

"It's not normal not to have dandruff. Maybe there's something wrong with him."

"Well, maybe you just can't see it from here. Let's get closer and find out."

"Okay. Oh look! he's scratching his head. He must have dandruff after all. Now I'm in love, too!"

1010. **Real Life #2**.

"Don't you love the smell of a girl in a sweat?"

"I wouldn't know. Every time Sally even begins to perspire, she runs off to the shower, and then really lays on the deodorant. Sometimes I think that girl has been wired backwards."

"Oh, she probably just wants to smell good for you—to please you. The right perfume properly cooked on a woman's skin is a real delight, you know."

"But sometimes I'd like to smell the woman, not the perfume."

1011. **Real Life #3**.

"Wait a minute; that's wrong."

"Wrong? What do you mean, 'wrong'? *Me* wrong? That's impossible. In fact, how dare you—"

"Well, look here."

"Oh, no! It's true! I *am* wrong! imperfect! defective! I've made a mistake! *failed!* How can I pronounce it? How can I even think it? How can I ever face the world again? Oh, wrong! wrong! Why me? Oh, why was I ever born, why made to crawl upon the earth and be wrong? The moment of horror has come and destruction is mine. How can I live from day to day knowing that I've made a mistake, that *I have been wrong*, failed, that I have embraced, kissed, believed an error? Yes, that error has passed through my lips with full assent in my stupid, ignorant, wrong belief! And what of others? Who will associate with me now; who will look at me with anything but loathing, contempt, and utter detestation? Who will speak my polluted name without an oath, without spitting and grinding the spittle into the ground with his foot? I will be used as an example to frighten children in every school, and as an object of laughter and scorn in every bar—no, I will be hunted out of society, driven into the deserts and mountains to live with the wild beasts, to dwell with snakes and scorpions and insects as loathsome as myself, or perhaps to be shunned by them, too! Oh how, oh why could I have done it? What made me wrong, fail? Oh, I can't stand it!"

1012. "May you have enough happiness to make you grateful and enough sorrow to make you kind." —Traditional Wedding Benediction

1013. The conclusion of my dissertation: Christianity is the only rational and objective solution to the problem of human life.

1014. When we have only one candle, we put it near a mirror to make it look like two. When we have two candles, we do not need a mirror.

1015. "Man was made to walk the earth and be wrong."

"And woman to remind him of it?"

"No, woman to love him anyway. For only in the perception that one is fallible and yet lovable can one be both humble and happy."

1016. The eraser on a pencil teaches a wise man all he needs to know about humility.

1017. Take care when you look upon what you are not permitted to touch or when you touch what you are not permitted to possess.

1018. **Real Life #4.**

"Did you notice that throughout the presentation to our clients Miss Jones stayed dry under the arms?"

"Yes, she looked cool and calm."

"That's right. She wasn't the least bit nervous. That means she didn't care whether we got the contract or not."

"I don't think we need employees like that."

"Me either. Let's fire her tomorrow."

1019. Anyone can look, and many can think. But only a very few can look and think at the same time.

1020. A stick hurts for an hour, but words can hurt for years. — Proverb

1021. There is a pathetic fallacy of people, where we invest others with the emotions we feel, or with emotions we think they ought to feel.

1022. Most truth, having long been known, is not very original. It is not new. Is it therefore to be spurned? Is it to be ignored because it is obvious, never mentioned again? Error repeats itself constantly, blaringly, forcefully. Why not truth?

1023. Man—passionate dust and a soul.

1024. If I have a Ph.D. or can write epics, but do not have love, I am just an empty beer can or a blowing paper. —1 Corinthians 13:1 (Doax Version)

1025. Why are people so attracted by the paint on the surface of life?

1026. They mistake the ornaments of life for life itself.

>   Of inner truth we find few care to know
>   Whose eyes are dazzled by the outside show.

1027. "Experience is the schoolmaster of fools." —Livy
Well, then, it was tailor-made for the human race.

1028. Do you think Jesus wore designer tunics?

1029. Only the happiness that makes God happy can make man happy.

1030. Man's body is a marvel of engineering, but woman's body is a work of art. A thinking girl is an idea you can touch, an idea you can kiss. An intelligent woman is thinking art.

1031. Life is so short, and yet we spend most of it waiting for time to pass.

1032. Children have a way of clarifying our lifestyles because they imitate our actions and habits without our self-deceit and hypocrisy. Many parents who live a greasy and tawdry life pretend to be surprised and offended when their children do the same.

1033. If we are really such rational creatures, why is it that we can talk ourselves into anything we want?

1034. **Self Confidence**.
"Marla, will you marry me?"
"Yes."
"What do you mean, 'yes'?"
"Yes, I will marry you."
"No, wait a minute. I mean marry me like having a wedding and living together and having children and stuff."
"I know. And I said, 'yes.'"
"Are you sure?"
"Of course. I love you."
"You love me!?"
"Sure."
"Are you sure? Love?"
"Of course."
"But why?"
et cetera

1035. What you pretend today you will believe tomorrow. You become what you do. Action leads to belief.

1036. May your words always have meaning.

1037. If men really knew how few women marry for love, the sound of crashing egos would deafen the world.

1038. How many times do we imagine ourselves giving them a kiss on the forehead when in reality we are sticking bamboo under their fingernails?

1039. People don't change as much as our perceptions of them do. But that's all right, because they were never what we thought they were to begin with.

1040. You is like you talks. — Proverb

1041. People complain about obscurity, bombast, and academic affectation and yet they regard clear writing as simplistic and superficial.

1042. The wind blows and you lose a branch from a tree. But the loss of the branch makes a gain in firewood. Thus are adversities often accompanied by benefits.

1043. Your project has had a small beginning? Remember that God stormed the universe by putting a baby on a pile of straw.

[January 1, 1983; age 33]

1044. One of our most common mistakes is neglecting to take reality into account.

1045. Roofing tar melts about 420 degrees and bursts into flame a little over 500 degrees. Life is like that. Work to stay melted, but don't burn up.

1046. Before you accuse your enemy of being a filthy person, be sure your spectacles are clean.

1047. The promise of technology is often much greater than its fulfillment. When a machine doesn't do what it's supposed to, we are disappointed; when a person doesn't do what he's supposed to, we are angry. We are thus more polite to machines than to people.

1048. Recently I saw a refuse truck racing down the freeway on the way to the dump. The whole concept of speeding garbage is certainly ripe for philosophical investigation, but in this case I simply wonder why the driver was in a hurry. Perhaps haste itself is the goal rather than the method, thus making trash the means to the end.

1049. People who give free advice should always offer a money back guarantee.

1050. A 50-50 marriage is hugging with one arm and kissing with one lip, expecting your spouse to supply the rest.

1051. A well-known truth is that there is no necessary connection between definition and understanding. Why then do we run around pigeon holing everything and then acting as if there is nothing more to be said? Many times when someone expresses wonder, interest, or amazement at something (a beautiful quartz crystal, for example), someone else will dump a definition or name on it and then act as if such a revelation should eliminate all feelings. "Why, that's just quartz—mere silicon dioxide; it's very common." You can define a flower or butterfly, but do you understand the thing you define? And isn't the same thing true with people? Why are we so anxious to put a label on everyone we meet? Do we feel safer if we can put everyone into a particular box?

1052. "Aren't you disappointed that you couldn't find the thing you were looking for?" a young man asked Darxul one day.

"I knew a wise man once," Darxul replied. "His greatest curse was, 'May you get everything you want.'"

"But if that was his curse, what was his blessing?"

"His blessing was, 'May the Lord bring you what you need.'"

1053. One does not argue for keeping a dead branch because it is a *large* dead branch: it must be cut off regardless of its size.

1054. **Principles of Creativity**.

1. To combine things not seen as combinable.

2. To associate very diverse things in ways that clarify them. The use of simile, metaphor, and other such associative devices.

3. To distinguish between two things thought the same. To show a fine differentiation or discrimination.

4. To extend or apply something known to further reaches.

5. To change something known to make it something new.

6. To ask or imagine, "What if?" Thus, what if trees could fly? What if smells had color?

1055. The expectation of gratitude is the first mistake of the human heart; the hope of reciprocated love is the second.

1056. When you discover that you lack a particular piece of knowledge, you can either supply the lack by learning something or you can discover some sophisticated way to hide your ignorance.

1057. In this phantasmagoric concatenation of perceptual phenomena known as life, most people are asleep, too pleased with their own dreams to wake; while those who are awake are unwilling to oxidize the metabolites of insanity because the thrill of delusion is more welcome than the stillness of truth. Who will carry a flag to the top of a hill when no one stands by to applaud? We dream dreams, and put ourselves into them, and believe them, and go mad because our egos are hungry. We want to be loved, and we are not loved.

1058. So love is a cure for all the intentional madnesses of life. Except that our egos are hungrier than any merely real, deep, true, and profound love can cure. Except sometimes.

1059. So the Christian should be the sanest man of all, for he knows that God loves him.

1060. The only burden men carry and wish it heavier is a golden one. No matter how weighted down by riches, they all wish for more.

1061. Ah, desire. We want not just the one piece of fruit needed to satisfy our physical appetites, but all the fruit on the tree to satisfy our imaginary appetites. And we want the tree, too—no, the whole orchard where the tree grows. And yes, we want the farmer's house and his virgin daughter as well.

A drink from the well would satisfy us, but we want title to every drop of rain that falls upon the earth.

1062. Imagine that you read ten statements, knowing that nine are true and that one is false, but not knowing which is which. How many of them would you believe? Even though there is a nine-to-one chance that a particular statement will be true, the false statement tinctures the whole batch. A little leaven leavens the whole lump. Do you now see why there can be no compromise with falsehood or evil?

1063. It's hard enough driving uphill on a muddy road in the dark, but when people keep shooting your tires out, too, only then do you realize the true difficulty of pursuing an idea.

1064. A closed book is only a piece of wood. — Proverb

1065. A cracked bell can sound loud or soft, fast or slow. But it can never sound whole. — Proverb

1066. Only the humble can feel wonder. And so we see that pride spoils half the enjoyment of life.

1067. The water is running under the bridge even when we are not looking.

1068. The worst people in the world are not those who stand up for evil, for wherever evil is clear it can be opposed and resisted. The worst people are those who try to blur the distinction between good and evil, and who work to mingle them.

1069. Every wise man knows that example is better than precept, but he also knows that talking is easier than doing.

1070. You have lost nothing if you haven't lost God. — Proverb

1071. If you want to feel rich, call your friends and enjoy what you have. If you want to feel poor, go to the marketplace and see what you lack.

1072. Evil is more easily prevented than cured. — Proverb.

1073. **A Gathering of Proverbs Not to be Lost.**
- All things are difficult before they are easy.
- Almost and Nearly save many a lie.
- Just as men test gold, so gold tests men.
- Choose a wife rather by your ear than by your eye.
- He is not poor who has little, but he who desires much.
- If the counsel be good, no matter who gave it.
- If the staff be crooked, the shadow cannot be straight.
- If the lion's skin cannot, the fox's shall.
- In the husband wisdom, in the wife gentleness.
- It is lawful to learn even from an enemy.
- More have repented speech than silence.

1074. Opinion rules the world, and Truth is permitted to attend her highness only if Truth happens to agree with her.

1075. **Another Basket of Proverbs.**
- The thin end of the wedge is to be feared.
- Time is a file that wears and makes no noise.
- Truth remains truth to the end of the argument.
- Two things a man should never be angry at are what he can help and what he cannot help.
- Who will not be ruled by the rudder must be ruled by the rock.
- Without danger we cannot get beyond danger.
- Zeal without knowledge is fire without light.

1076. A prayer before reading the Bible: Lord, bless the reading of your precious and wonderful word. Send your Holy Spirit to me to illuminate my mind so that I can comprehend fully what you are saying to me. Help me to know your will for my life and to remember your eternal truths. Amen.

1077. Almost nothing *really* matters, but everything matters.

1078. The wisdom or folly of your life results not so much from what you look at as from what you see.

1079. We are the trees that want to live in the Land of Always Sunshine, but we must live in the Land of Sometimes Rain if we are to bear fruit.

1080. How desperately most people want to live a life of meaningful clichés.

1081. How easy it is to forget the lessons we don't want to remember. And when a rule interferes with our hopes, wishes, desires, greed, lust, or vanity, how quickly we forget it, ignore it, or declare its invalidity.

1082. Thou shalt not covet thy neighbor's sports car, nor his speedboat, nor his hot tub, nor anything that is thy neighbor's. —Exodus 20:17 (Doax version)

[January 1, 1984; age 34]

1083. Better is an inflatable boat with him who loves the Lord, than a hundred-foot yacht and unbelief. —Proverbs 15:16 (Doax version)

1084. The threat of hell or the promise of heaven is very seldom the basis for a conversion or for belief in Christ. Rather the typical conversion results when someone finally understands that the love God has for him is real. We believe by discovering the truth of the love of God. And for those who think about such things, we believe because of the rationality of the answers to questions otherwise unanswerable. So fear and future hope are less powerful operators than the immediacy of the Gospel—

how Christ can affect our lives and satisfy our minds now.

1085. Christianity is to be accepted not as a guarantee of happiness or pleasure, but because it is true; it is a necessary part of reality, as well as the path to everlasting life.

1086. The greatest freedom of the human soul is found in the stability, solidity, and objectivity of Christianity.

1087. The human experience is a perpetual delusion not because reality lacks the strength to overcome the mind, but because people desire delusion and work hard to maintain it. People have emotional investments in their ideas and perceptions; they "know" that something must be true or false and will not have it otherwise. Few ever argue or learn with their minds; they are in the habit of thinking and being convinced through feeling and desire because that is what delusion requires. To think with the mind would end many delusions.

Jesus said, "You shall know the truth, and the truth shall make you free," but most people do not want to be made free or to know the truth. They would rather have the security and comfort of their own delusions, which have been constructed to permit an easy, selfish, and most of all, ego-propping life. Thus, too many of us search for evidence not to bring us truth, but to support our delusions and pet beliefs.

1088. You can say "alas" and "too bad" ten times, but things are still the same.

1089. Why are things admired? A few things are honored because they are worthy—superior, artistic, valuable, useful. But many more things are admired because they are new, or perhaps just different. Welded junk gains admiration on these grounds. The biggest reason for admiration, though, is also the silliest—things are admired simply because other people admire them. The public relations people cannot believe their good fortune at this quirk of human nature. The logicians with their *ad populum* fallacy are kicked aside in the rush to take part in the worship of the popular.

1090. One of the most fundamental human needs is to feel appreciated. And a second is to feel needed or wanted. Yet how seldom do we take the time to show others that we need and appreciate them?

1091. Pride is the biggest obstacle to faith, to friendship, to loyalty. We will do "anything" for someone else or for God—but only if it doesn't humble us. A man wanted to study philosophy under Diogenes. Diogenes gave him a dead fish to carry and told him to follow him. But the man out of shame threw the fish down and went away. (This from Diogenes Laertius, VI.36.) How many—or rather, how few—of us would carry a dead fish around in public, even for a day, to prove our loyalty and devotion to a girlfriend, boyfriend, spouse, or to God himself? And yet what is the burden of carrying a dead fish? It is only our proud hearts that make it a burden. "People will laugh at me," we say. Are we not willing to be laughed at for the sake of love or truth? Are we really so disgustingly petty, selfish, and proud? Yes, we are.

1092. "Here's a girl for you—intelligent, devoted, sensitive, good sense of humor, agreeable, thoughtful, fantastic personality, kind hearted and generous, giving. She can sing, play, write; will be a companion in all your studies and endeavors, supportive—"
    "Wait."
    "But the list goes on."
    "I don't care. Is she beautiful?"
    "No."
    "Then forget it."
    "Well, then here's a beautiful girl. However, she's proud, critical, materialistic, bossy, selfish, stuffy, thoughtless, cold, vain—"
    "Never mind. I'll take her."

1093. I say that beauty is not important, but if I should marry, that opinion will be discounted. If I marry a plain girl, people will say, "He's trying to rationalize his lot" or "He's trying to make his wife feel good." If I marry a beauty, they will say, "I see the hypocrite managed to ignore his own advice" or "That's easy for him to say now that he's got a gorgeous babe."

1094. Just what is your place in the sun? Mine is W 117° 31′ 28″ by N 33° 49′ 30″ as of January 11, 1984.

1095. About to meet a salesman, Darxul opened *The Book of One Hundred Lies* and read:
    23. Of course it will go up in value.
    24. No, there is no obligation.
    25. Listen, I know what I'm talking about.

1096. Diogenes Laertius records that someone said to one of the Greek philosophers, "Isn't it a shame that roses have thorns?" And the philosopher replied, "On the contrary, isn't it a blessing that thorns have roses?"

1097. When money enters the argument, morality is usually asked to leave.

1098. Dear Lord, make my love larger than my pride.

1099. NOW ON SALE: HUMAN Was 1000 droblebs in our Fall catalog, now only 799 droblebs each. Every human features
    + Modern design
    + Moves on own power
    + Waterproof
    + Self cleaning
    + Self starting
    + Never needs batteries

Comes in a choice of style and color, and available plain or decorated (decorated, add 25 droblebs). (Note: As with all biological units, Human is sold AS IS. Purchase book #28736-G, "How to Operate a Human," and book #394773-FN, "Care and Feeding of the Human Organism," for proper instructions and maintenance.)

When ordering, specify size (short, medium, tall), style (female [has bulges on chest] or male [has hair in armpits]), and color (tanpink, light brown, dark brown, ebony). Orders subject to stock on hand. Limited availability. Use your GalaxyCharge.

1100. No one wants to be loved too little — or too much.

1101. "The more the grape vine struggles, the better the wine." So say the viticulturists and enologists, but are they talking about plants or about the human heart?

1102. The worship of external appearance has finally joined with conspicuous consumption to give us the detailed labels we now find on cars. It's not enough to have the brand of our clothes on the outside, or the brand of the car. Now we must give all the impressive details about the expensive features we paid extra for. "3.8 Liter V-6" says one label. "InterCooler Turbo" says another. "Fuel Injection OHC" says another. Maybe the price and option stickers should be etched into the glass to supply a permanent brag about everything the car has on it.

1103. How impressionable, even suggestible, people are! It's almost shocking to see people adopt or change attitudes or beliefs about ideas, other people, and even themselves, just on the basis of what someone says to them. Even though the proverb, "Saying so is not making so," is one of the fundamental truths we are all supposed to know, not many people seem to remember it. And for them, apparently, saying so *is* making so.

1104. You know this already, but I'll say it again. Persevere, take risks, expect failures, learn from them, leave them behind you. Jack London received six hundred rejection slips before his work finally began to catch on. Then he became very popular. Can you, who desire to serve God, give up any sooner? Those are not periods the world is throwing at you, only commas.

1105. The knowledge of something new comes to us as a general notion (says Diogenes Laertius, discussing the stoics, VII.42). But knowledge also comes to us through comparison; we are always learning by thinking to ourselves, "Oh, it seems to be sort of like. . . ." We begin to learn something by generalization and comparison, so that we begin with only vague and inexact ideas. Then, as we learn, we refine, distinguish, and discriminate. Exact knowledge, then, comes from a process of refinement. It is probably not possible to grasp exactness at the outset. Learning is a process of comparison, contrast, and differentiation as much as it is a process of apprehension.

1106. Before he opened the official document, Darxul glanced into *The Book of One Hundred Lies* and read:
     26. These are just voluntary guidelines. There's no danger of their becoming mandatory, and there's no penalty if you don't observe them.
     27. We want this information only for statistical purposes. It will not be used against you.

1107. The status-quo-ites are still with us, affirming that "Whatever is, is right." We often hear rationalizations for evil from them, as when someone is murdered, they say, "Don't you suppose he provoked it? What was he doing out at midnight, anyway?" Or when someone is drowned in a flood, "They shouldn't have been living there."

1108. If you can convince a slave that he is free in his bondage, he will refuse to be genuinely set free. So the humanist establishment continues to exclaim, "You are free, you are free!" and to promote ever more selfishness. Freedom is equated with anarchy or at least with license, so that people will continue to be slaves to fad, whim, passion, public opinion, and so on. But there is no freedom without rules. There can be no freedom where everyone selfishly pursues his own ends; there can be only fraud, theft, rape, killing, deceit, moral auctioneering, oppression — dangers and restraints of every kind.

1109. Lessons From the Olympics (1980).

1. Consistency is much more important than unrepeatable, though absolutely magnificent, accomplishment. The competition, like life, is a series of contests wherein the participant must prove himself excellent many times over before he can become the champion.

2. Most lose. Even the eventual gold medalists lose a lot in their progress toward the top. And for every gold medalist, there are thousands of losers of finals, semi-finals, heats, qualifying races. Think of the regional competitions, the local meets, the school tryouts.

3. Chance, even among the best in the world, is a large factor in determining the winner. A breeze, a broken shoelace, just feeling slightly off in the morning, a pebble at the starting blocks. Yes, the saying is that chance favors those who are prepared, and of course that is true. But still, so many times the difference between the "absolutely greatest" and "absolutely not the greatest" is just some small quirk.

4. Minuscule differences in time divide the winners from the losers in many competitions. Is a hundredth of a second really significant? We should have clocks that measure only in whole seconds, and give equal medals to all those with the same times. It's silly — even sick — to divide between gold and silver, or between bronze and nothing, for a hundredth of a second.

5. Art is important, even over technical perfection, for the spectator. There's an esthetic to sport that should not be overlooked.

6. Even the best lose, crash, fall, or otherwise botch it very often. This is probably the most important lesson. Even the champ fails, makes mistakes, has poor judgment, and suffers bad days. No one is always up or always on top. No one is always the champ.

7. Someone always comes in last in each event.

1110. Why must we always be reminded that virtue and piety rather than charm should be the basis for choice in a friend or spouse? Because we always forget? Why do we forget? Because half our hearts want us to forget. Without reflection, our passionate hearts, if left alone, will always choose charm over goodness, intelligence, even over genuine kindness, humanity, selflessness, and humility. The proud, selfish charmer has hundreds of unthinking followers all trying to make themselves unhappy while believing they are seeking happiness.

1111. First marriage is often a blind and desperate attempt to fulfill utterly selfish and impossible romantic notions by requiring the spouse to be an ideal person alien to his real nature. People marry their own imaginations and then try to force the poor, real spouse into the mold. Second marriages are at once more realistic, more human, and involve more giving of oneself. The Christian must be right the first time, since he is permitted only one spouse.

1112. Thank you, Lord, for giving me being, and for giving me an opportunity to serve you in this world. Thank you for a savior to forgive me of my sins and to redirect my life into profitable and worthy paths. And thank you, dear Lord, for loving me, poor creature that I am, for valuing me and for letting me know that you care. Amen.

1113. Man is the image of God and a book is the image of man. Therefore, a book may possess a reflected divinity.

1114. A visual representation of an idea is powerful and affecting, the more so the closer it comes to photographic realism. Thus all art and illustrations, but especially motion pictures and plays, are powerfully affecting because they seem so much like real life. The motion picture can affect belief, much more so than any collection of arguments. People believe what they see, even though the plot, characters, and circumstances are all false and rigged to serve the end of the writer and producer. The realistic portrayal of fantasy makes the imagination seem real and possible, but putting wish fulfillment safely apart from the problems and complications of reality can be dangerous for those who will go outside the theater and try to adjust their behavior by what they have seen.

1115. The current method of arguing for something is to use the *ad populum* appeal: "Get with it." "This is the popular idea." The current method of arguing against something is to laugh at it, show that it is unpopular or square or nerdish (that squares and nerds believe it or like it), and to show that it is not pragmatic — here's a situation where it doesn't work.

1116. "Wonder implies the desire to learn," says Aristotle (*Rhetoric*, 1.11). So people who will not allow themselves to feel wonder are also unwilling to learn. Wonder is an admission of humility. Once again we see the damage wreaked by pride.

1117. Aristotle also says that "the failure to perceive is a sign of slighting" (*Rhetoric*, 2.2). Not only do people "deliberately forget" (2 Peter 3:5), but they deliberately refuse to become aware of some things, as a pretense to superiority.

1118. Almost the whole sum of our life is the continuous battle against pride and its effects. Selfishness and even greed are traceable to it. How strong is pride? Read Revelation 16:10-11: "Men gnawed their tongues in agony and cursed the God of heaven because of their pains and sores, but they refused to repent and glorify him." The human heart will endure anything to avoid humbling itself. What is it that has given a crumb of dust such an attitude?

1119. How ambivalent we are toward choice! Choice is an opportunity and a burden, a freedom and an anxiety. We demand choice and rejoice in its possibilities, but often we flee from it or make a choice quickly just to get it over with. Ah, the glory and terror of alternatives.

1120. Is a bridge useless when no one is crossing it?

1121. Workers operating dangerous machinery have been known to cut off their fingers because of a momentary lapse of attention, even though they are concentrating as fully as they can. Can you then be offended when a student's attention wanders from one of your lectures?

1122. The typical American is remarkably out of shape and underexercised, yet his greatest goal in life is to find a parking space near the door. Nothing makes him happier than saving twenty steps.

1123. Silence is also an opinion. — Proverb

1124. In our enthusiasm to tell of the goodness of Christianity we sometimes forget that it is also true.

1125. A barrier made of paper is just as strong as one made of concrete ten feet thick, until you attack it. That's why courage rather than strength makes heroes.

1126. We treat other people the way postmen treat letters. We look at the outside and decide what little predetermined slot or cubbyhole to put them in. We admire the official-looking ones and scorn the ones with poor handwriting. We laugh when the stamp is crooked or upside down. We sort the letters and count the totals, and later mention the numbers to our friends. But we never look inside because that's someone else's business.

1127. Committees labor on the cutting edge of irrationality.

1128. **The Committee**.
   "The item of business today is to decide upon a suitable ve-

hicle for our messenger to take blueprints from the office to the job site."

"How about a Toyota? They're good cars."

"I don't mean to sound like a Chevy salesman, but Chevy is a really great buy and a lot of people are going with it."

"We should definitely go with a van."

"I don't think we should under buy. Our needs may increase and we want to be ready for the future. I think we should get a double trailer truck with a turbocharged diesel."

"You know, Cadillac is a good value. They are solid cars."

"But we have only a few blueprints and they would fit easily into a trunk or back seat."

"Cars are an old technology. We don't want to buy into the past. The latest thing now is the jet helicopter."

"Mercedes makes a really good automobile, durable, quiet, good resale value."

"How about a racing motorbike? They can go over 150 miles per hour, dodge traffic, and be parked anywhere. Besides, Kawasaki is offering a special price to corporations now."

"But we couldn't put our blueprint cases on a racing motorbike."

"Well, we could cut the blueprints up and put them under the seat."

"We should be thinking of the future here. We might want to start hauling parts to the site, and a dinky car or van might not be big enough. We ought to think seriously about getting a business jet—a Gulfstream II at least. Learjets are a bit small."

"No, we ought to go with a Sikorsky Skycrane helicopter if we want to haul I-beams and concrete to the site."

"By the way, how much money is budgeted for buying the vehicle?"

"Right now, nothing. We can't buy anything until we get the money."

"You know, Rolls Royce is a really well-respected automobile."

"I don't want to sound like a 747 salesman, but. . . ."

1129. **Love**.
    He: "I think you are a wonderful, high-quality girl."
    She: "I do, too."
    He: "Your skin is very soft."
    She: "Most skin is."
    He: "Would you like to have lunch with me?"
    She: "I'll let you know in a week."
    He: "This is a nice walk."
    She: "You know, I'm bored easily."
    He: "What do you plan to do when you graduate?"
    She: "Go to nursing school. I probably won't get married for a long time. I would like to meet a good-looking guy, though."

1130. To possess artificial intelligence, a computer must be able to do the following:
    1. understand metaphors and other figurative language.
    2. detect puns
    3. decipher ambiguities appropriately
    4. use context to determine the meaning of many words.
    5. determine mood and tone, as in irony, anger, humor.

[April, 1985; age 34]

1131. The assumptions one makes, whether in argument or description, constitute an attempt to establish a particular view as normative. Assumptions can thus be propagandistic.

1132. The Lord sends many odd experiences to cure us of faults that have resisted both our own reason and the repeated exhortation of others.

1133. Courage is not the opposite of fear. Courage is the power to act in spite of fear. The courageous are often very frightened.

1134. Trust is not the same as stability or security. It is a confidence of motives in the face of all circumstances and events. A person you trust may cause you pain, but you accept that pain in the belief that your good or ultimate good will result. Thus, trust is a confidence of *moral* motives.

1135. Of the 43 definitions of love, a good one might be this. Love is giving without the desire for return, the surrender of the self to others. It is caring for, caring about others. It is a motivation to good quite beyond any feelings of duty or obligation—which is why love is above the law. Love actively seeks needs in others and then responds to those needs. Love is understanding, forgiveness, compassion, generosity—because all of these are of the essence of giving.

And love, emotionally and romantically speaking, is also the admission of need, because to admit that you need another is a kind of self-surrender and even, yes, of giving.

1136. Darxul hung up the phone wearily and then added these to *The Book of One Hundred Lies*:

28. You're the first person who's ever complained about that. No one else is experiencing the problem.

29. Yes, that's coming very soon.

30. We really want to do it, but we just can't.

31. I know it's expensive, but you get what you pay for.

1137. Pythagoras defines friendship as "one soul in two bodies." Sometimes that poor, ripped apart soul in us finds its other half, and then how powerfully it desires to join itself together again.

1138. Many actions have multiple motives, including some unselfish and some selfish. But if the action is good and the major motive is good, that is as much as can be expected from a human being.

1139. **Administrative Stumbling Blocks.**

1. Some administrators idolize working documents, seeing them as fixed and rigid recipes rather than as guidelines to good and efficient administration. An old proverb tells us, "Young men know the rules, but old men know the exceptions." Know-

ing when to depart from or extend the guidelines is part of quality leadership.

2. Mechanical emergencies are attended to immediately and without thought, while human emergencies are rejected even after protracted consideration. Many companies boast that their employees are their best asset, but what is the practice? Millions for machines and peanuts for people? Tell this story to your administrator and see what he says:

"Hey boss! Leonardo Da Vinci is here and wants a job in R&D. Says he has some good ideas and will work for fifty K. We really don't want to miss this, huh?"

"Well, that certainly would be good to get such an excellent and creative person, but we just don't have the money in the budget. Sorry."

— Ten Minutes Later —

"Hey boss! The sewer just blew up! We'll need $50 thousand to fix it."

"Okay, get the men on it right away. I'll look in the contingency fund or in some account or even borrow the money. After all, this is an emergency."

The good administrator will say, "You know, there's something to that. Maybe we should rethink our idea of 'emergency.'" The mediocre administrator will say, "If Leonardo came in, we'd give him a job." And the lousy administrator will say, "You just don't understand the situation." The poor administrator reacts only to deficit needs; the good administrator will act upon opportunities to meet "needs" not yet discovered.

1140. Don't take no for an answer—at least not the first few times—if you are sure, or even suspect, that you are right. But be prepared for ultimate rejection.

1141. You can't reason someone out of a decision he was never reasoned into.

1142. To exercise your abilities to the fullest, it is necessary to take risks. Risks sometimes pay off; they sometimes fail. Failure is a token that *something* was attempted. (And don't forget, as the girls say, "Always have plan B" in case your risk does fail.)

1143. Reality is always different from what we expect. That makes life interesting, exciting, and painful.

1144. Just as the body is weakened and subject to disease by abuse (standing in the rain, too much exertion), so too is the soul, when it is abused, by sinful acts or indulgences, or even by the roughness and crudeness of modern "culture."

1145. Some statements appear at first to be neither true nor false, or perhaps both true and false. Many of these statements are true only in a particular context or under special circumstances. A simple example would be, "This is the biggest book," when a certain book is the largest in the room. True in the context of the room, the statement would not be true in a different context where an even larger book exists.

Some more important examples include all the classic turn downs young ladies give when not interested in a date: I'm too tired; I have to wash my hair, I have too much homework. All of these may be true in the immediate context but are subject to change if the context is enlarged (that is, if a more attractive offer is made). A student once asked a girl at the beach to play Frisbee with him and she said she was too tired. He then said he was a medical student and she suddenly developed enough energy to play.

The professional world makes the same kind of true-only-in-context assertions: I don't have time for any new projects; we just don't have the money.

1146. Only time reveals the importance of a person or event on our lives. The question, "Is he an influence?" is hard to answer; but, "Was he an influence?" is easier.

1147. Most pigeonholes we form for other people rely upon too rigid a notion of the adjectives we use to construct them. Is Fred "generous"? Yes or no. But we ought to take into account the degree, the kind, and the time. That is, how generous, what kind of generosity, and when? The same is true for every other description or characteristic.

1148. We think of ourselves as unique individuals and we think of everyone else as a type. Some people even want to marry what would best be described as a generic handsome man or a generic beautiful woman. But people are not interchangeable. They are not even very much types. People are all individuals. Thus we see the danger of seeing others as labels—doctor, preacher, teacher, mechanic, executive, whatever.

1149. Perelman and Olbrechts-Tyteca say, "Abstract values . . . when carried to extremes, are irreconcilable: it is impossible to reconcile, in the abstract, such virtues as justice and love" (79). In many such cases, there exists no hierarchy for those two values, either. Is justice or mercy more important? The rights of parents or the rights of children? Only in a concrete application of value can reconciliation or hierarchy be produced.

1150. Strangeness is truer than fiction.

1151. Inside every cat is a tiger, and inside every woman is a princess.

1152. God is not a toy. Why do we treat him like one, trying to make him dance or sit or follow our imagination? You are beginning to grow spiritually mature when you stop trying to teach God, when you realize he already knows what you were going to say. And he knows a few things you don't know, too.

1153. To say that "people believe what they see" is true and sad but not new or profound. But to note that "people see what they believe" constitutes a real insight. For there is no such thing as unfiltered or completely objective perception.

1154. Often, love is hard work. But sometimes it's as easy as breathing.

1155. A student entering college as a freshman knows everything. When he graduates as a senior, he doesn't know anything. This process we call education. For when someone realizes how little he really knows, then he is well on the way to becoming educated.

1156. They are building a very elegant mansion on a foundation of Jello.

1157. Man invented the alarm clock and thereby showed that his mind is greater than his body. He has the will to control the longings of his body for sleep and inactivity.

1158. Our whole society, both religious and secular, has as a major operational principle that emotional response, feeling, or persuasion is more real and of higher value than intellectual conviction. We have given up commitment love for romantic love; the preacher aims to work up his audience rather than to instruct it; an attempt to analyze a personal relationship is condemned as "sterile"; many people decry "mere intellectual knowledge" as being inferior to "real experience," by which they often mean emotional experience. The problem with feelings is that they are a hundred times more easily fooled or manipulated than the mind, even in substantially educated people.

1159. We are too much slaves of the formulations of others. We call the schema of others "truth" instead of an "interpretation" or even "opinion" or "working definition." When, for example, someone says, "There are sixteen personality types," we take that for scientific fact. But what has happened to fact when the next fad arrives, claiming that there are four or thirty-three types?

1160. **Overheard exchange**.

Fred's been with the company for ten years and he's never made a mistake."

"Oh? In that case, fire him."

1161. Only the risk takers are truly free. —Proverb

1162. When you marry you do not marry a thing or even a person, but a personality process. People change through time, and even from day to day. That's one reason why statements like, "You're not the person I married" are so idiotic. The second reason those statements are idiotic is that most people marry their own imaginations rather than a real other person in the first place.

1163. The more you get, the more you have; the more you give, the more you are. —Proverb

1164. Blessed are the flexible, for they shall not be broken. —Proverb

1165. Time lost cannot be regained. And yet people who would never waste money waste the days and years of their lives without a thought, often just waiting for time to pass. Remember that every day, you are spending your life. Spend it on something of value.

1166. Literature: the home of civilization, culture, and wisdom, where truth has married art, where ideas frolic in the sunshine and hold the hands of love and beauty, an orchard of sweetness and light, the mind's whetstone and the soul's jacuzzi.

1167. Why is it that nature shows on television—those that cover the phenomena and beauty of the natural world—so often seem to be preoccupied with death and guilt? "Here we see the fierce lion chomping on the guts of the helpless gazelle, and it is the fault of that worst of predators, man, that this scene is not as common as it once was."

1168. The Bible is the true recipe, but most people want to put in only the ingredients they like and in the proportions they choose, so that the resulting dishes — their lives — are often distasteful or even poisonous.

1169. "When I get married, I plan to give fifty percent and take fifty percent."

"Then your marriage is already doomed."

"Why? Don't you believe that marriage is a give and take situation?"

"Not at all. Marriage is a give situation. Unless both partners give a hundred percent each, the relationship is in trouble. And when someone starts thinking about taking, the relationship is in trouble then, too. Much of the giving in a relationship is invisible to the receiver, so that most spouses think that they are giving much more than they are taking. Once they start to put numbers on the situation, some attorney is soon going to buy a new Mercedes."

1170. Your students may not read the textbooks you assign, but they will read the book of your life — whether you want them to or not.

1171. Q. Why does college last four years?

A. It takes four years just to learn how ignorant you are.

1172. When you're young and foolish, you do some foolish things; when you're old and foolish, you get completely ridiculous.

1173. We see everywhere unhappy people — people who have lived too quantitatively, without regard for quality. The very best doesn't come in truck loads.

1174. When all has been said and done, a lot will have been said and not much done.

1175. Actions speak louder than words, but hey, is this a library or what?

1176. Humans value accuracy and meticulousness, yet they can create a machine that is far more exact in performing repeated, dumb tasks (such as numbering Glimmerings!) than its designers.

1177. Talk is cheap and most people like to get a lot for their money.

1178. God never closes.

1179. I have made thousands of mistakes in my life, thank God.

1180. "Every man uses everything according to the opinion which he has about it," says Epictetus (I.iii). How important, then, it is to have right opinions about other people, especially those close to you—your friend, your spouse, your child. How powerful are they who shape the attitudes of others about things and about people. And do note that we behave not according to what the thing or person is, but only according to our opinion about it. Let us then strive to adjust our opinion to match the essence.

1181. "For what else is tragedy than the perturbations of men who value externals?" —Epictetus (I.iv)

1182. Would a woman rather have flowers or a frying pan for Valentine's Day? Would a man rather have flowers or a pair of pliers for Valentine's Day? Do women value emotional metaphors more than men, or do women instead value certain culturally endowed vehicles more than others, and in ways and degrees different from men?

1183. There are no locks in heaven. Do you know what that means? Do you know what it means to have keys on earth?

1184. People have more need of models than of critics or even instructors.

1185. Most of the actions of life are based on beliefs, hopes, guesses — sometimes on judgments of probability — rather than on certainties. When one is moving forward, the certainties are behind him.

1186. As the Chinese proverb says, "The only way to keep an action secret is not to do it."

1187. Love is a decision to place value on another and to give to that person. In other words, love is a commitment to the welfare of others. It spills over into emotion and the wells of feeling are continually refilled by it.

1188. The creative thinker has the ability to see as a benefit or advantage some property seen by others as a defect. The "bad" thing about super glue is that it will glue your skin together — so keep it off your fingers. The benefit is that gluing skin together is just what surgeons need. The "defective" glue that holds weakly was just the answer for a temporary stick on, like the Post-It note.

1189. Your student doesn't want to know what you know; he wants to understand the way he sees you understand.

1190. The quality of all the lives you touch is directly affected — even shaped — by what you know and don't know.

1191. **The Goals of Education.**
　　1. How to think.
　　　　a. analysis and comprehension, the study of logic, se-

mantics, the techniques of slanting, what is fair.

b. how to argue, the creation of good arguments backed by substantial, relevant reasons

c. thinking creatively, and a connection to #4, below, creative problem solving

2. How to learn.

a. reading/studying with perception and intelligence

b. learning how to listen well, attending to the other person's statements

c. determining the teacher's or author's worldviews, theses, biases, preconceptions, ontology, ethos, reliability, and assumptions

3. Growth in wisdom and culture.

a. the truths of human nature, behavior, motivation

b. art, literature, music

4. How to solve problems.

a. stimulating an eagerness to seek out and face and attack problems and difficulties

b. strategies for solving problems

5. Values and value articulation.

a. the inculcation of ethics, good values, morals (linked with wisdom, #3 above)

b. the ability to articulate a coherent and persuasive ethics (The inability to articulate intelligently one's beliefs is a chronic problem. Why exactly, do you believe as you do and why should I believe that way also?)

6. Exposure to the great ideas.

a. The broadening of knowledge and experience and the awareness of possibility and truth contestants

7. The fostering of independence of intellect and personality.

a. training one to learn, discover, think, act on one's own accord without hand holding by someone else

Classes in the New University:

1. Foundations. Study of ontological, epistemological, axiological, and revelational questions and assumptions for the formation of a credible basis of reality, truth, and value.

2. Logic (informal), including induction, deduction, semantics, constructing good arguments, analytic thinking

3. Rhetoric (classical), with special emphasis on the categories of metaphor

4. Ethics, emphasizing the construction, criticism, and defense of general and particular systems and positions.

5. Philosophy, an intro to philosophical questions not covered in foundations and an intro to great thinkers and their works

6. Problem solving and creative thinking, how to

7. Wisdom literature, and what makes us wise

8. Great ideas. Study of great ideas.

9. Comparative religion, to see just what the rest of the world thinks (including agnosticism, atheism, humanism, and nothings).

10. Christianity/Biblical studies, for solid basis in the Book and the Faith.

1192. If you allow someone to believe something that you know to be false, you are lying to that person.

[August, 1987; age 36]

1193. We spend a lot of time asking God to level the mountain in front of us when we should instead be asking him to make us mountain climbers.

1194. Many people are difficult to teach because they are ready to learn only what they imagine is to be learned, only what fits in readily with their preconceived notions and with their expectations. When you try to teach something that conflicts with expectations, you will be greeted with laughter or hostility.

1195. There is a difference between experience and knowledge: many people live thrill-ride existences without ever learning anything. There is also a difference between knowledge and wisdom: I recall hearing of a man who could remember every meal he had ever eaten, and of a woman who had read 9,000 paperback romances. Neither of these people had any wisdom out of the ordinary. And yet there is a connection between experience and knowledge and between knowledge and wisdom.

1196. We must be careful not to allow our thinking to be controlled by the metaphors of others. Metaphors are highly attractive; our minds seize upon them and trace them through, conforming our perceptions and thoughts to the parts of the image.

1197. One of the principal signs of knowledge is the ability to ask questions. Questions reveal a recognition of one's ignorance (and thus a knowledge of oneself unhampered by ego) and an intelligent interaction with some knowledge environment.

1198. How many people are prisoners of the ordinary. You can readily discover this by the total astonishment, disbelief, and even angry rejection you'll face when you propose anything even slightly out of the ordinary. Incredulity and ridicule greet even the mildest ideas like putting whipping cream in coffee, eating chocolate covered prunes, making peanut butter and banana sandwiches, wearing tennis shoes with a suit. There is a bit too much sameness in society and our ideas of social acceptability are much too narrow.

[April, 1988; age 37]

1199. Most people want to be led but not dictated to. They enjoy the comfort of going with the flow of society, feeling its push or pull, but they don't want to feel forced. We are paradoxes of gregariousness and individualism, of sheep and eagles.

1200. Why were the old sailing ships decorated with filigrees and moldings and with carvings of mermaids? Why were the old books illuminated with colorful drawings? Why were buildings covered with gothic decor? Why were common walking staffs carved and ornamented? Because esthetics were seen as a necessary part of life and business. People realized that life was enhanced by psychological enjoyment. There was not the ruthless utilitarianism we find today. Even hand tools, like scissors and knives, were engraved with patterns to make their use more enjoyable, though not more "effective." Buildings and ships and tools are used by the mind and heart and soul and not just by the body. The overemphasis on utility has impoverished our lives—we are starved esthetically in our concrete wastelands.

[August, 1988; age 37]

1201. Imitation is the flattest form of sincerity.

1202. "Success is the progressive realization of a worthy ideal." —Earl Nightingale, quoted in *Seeds of Greatness*. It's good to examine the definitions of abstract words like this—success, love, freedom—and to provide our own definitions. That way we won't be trapped or manipulated by long-accepted and long-unexamined definitions, definitions which may be thinking traps.

1203. Theology that doesn't become biography is wishful thinking.

[April, 1989; age 38]

1204. Invention is the mother of necessity. —Proverb

1205. Putting ideas in writing gives them an existence and a reality they do not have when spoken. They take upon them an authority. Reading ideas—statements about values, the *oughts* of behavior—gives a believability and persuasiveness to them. Many people in the past acted rightly because they read books telling them to act that way. Now people read books telling them to act foolishly.

1206. People are more often stupid than evil. So next time you see someone doing bad things, ask yourself thoughtfully, "Is he really evil, or just stupid?"

1207. Learning is a process that has to do with thinking as much as it does with experience. Mere information or experience does not necessarily result in learning or real knowledge. A person with twenty years' experience fixing cars could still be a terrible mechanic; some women's cooking never improves; some people with minds full of information or even values never can apply what they know. Thus, empiricism itself is limited by the ideas and thinking of people rather than by information gaps.

1208. Empiricism has two major limitations. First, many of the great issues and worthy considerations are not strictly subjectible to the empirical method. Questions about beauty, goodness, truth, art, the hunger of the soul, and so forth, do not lend themselves to an empirical investigation or proof. Second, the empirical method itself is not the objective, facts-only method we are sometimes told it is. Facts, evidence, details, proofs, all are subject to interpretation, theory, opinion, and so on. Thus, in some areas of reality we meet bigotry and narrowness in the guise of science and objective truth.

1209. What about empirical proof for the existence of God? The standard claim by many is, "I don't see a shred of evidence for the existence of God." I, on the other hand, see evidence every-where for his existence—in flowers, crystals, birds, butterflies, and so on. Our disagreement is over how to interpret these data, not on whether they exist or not.

1210. Both our sleeping and our waking dreams show us how much our minds and lives are products of our culture and expe-rience. Our sleeping dreams reflect, often in bizarre fashion, the events and worries of our lives, as well as the news and enter-tainment we subject ourselves to. We dream restlessly about drugs, mental patients, fires—whatever was on television that day. Our waking dreams are shaped by (1) our knowledge and (2) the values we've half-consciously assimilated from our culture.

1211. If, as I think, there are three aspects to God's will—his executive will, which is always done; his permissive will, which allows things to happen; and his directive will, which is what he wants us to do, but which we may refuse or reject—the question then becomes, How detailed is God's contact with our lives? How closely does he intervene? At what level of detail does he have a directive will for us? In other words, how are we to distinguish between his permissive and directive will, or between his executive and permissive will? How many of the small things does he do?

When we are served a good cup of coffee, meet a nice new person, or find a passage in a book we prayed for help in finding, did God do this or simply allow it to happen? When we say, "It was God's will" for either a good or bad event, do we mean permissive or executive? How much does God allow chance to determine events in our lives? Would anyone argue that he prescribes every parking place, the moment the Kleenex box gets empty, the insect bite on your arm?

A second question is, How do we distinguish between the whisper of the Holy Spirit and our own inner thoughts? Suppose you're on the way into a coffee shop. You see the newspaper rack and you hear an urging inside you, "Buy a newspaper," or "I should buy a newspaper." How can you know whether that's yourself or the Holy Spirit?

1212. All artists, but perhaps especially the Japanese, follow a method of studied asymmetry, randomness, seeming imperfection. They let the imagination complete lines or figures, let the imagination play with the design. In a series of parallel lines around a vase, the artist leaves some of the lines unfinished, broken. The gaps in the lines are part of the structure, part of the presentation as much as the lines themselves. Art should be suggestive as well as presentational.

1213. Many people are alive without a plan. They have no plans to reach long term goals (even if they have long term goals); all they have are unshaped dreams and a "someday" timetable. Many job applicants are quite embarrassed by the question, "Where do you see yourself in five years?"

1214. In the distant past a collection of varied opinions about reality was allowed. The ancient Greeks used to debate such opinions openly, as did later civilizations. Now, however, because of the tyrannical reign of empiricism, only one set of ideas can be allowed, because only one can be true and scientific. The fallacy of this attitude is that what is true and scientific is subject to interpretation and change. Empiricism is a method (and a limited one) that does not deliver us from subjectivity, opinion, a priori assumptions, ad hoc theory, or interpretation. Thus we have bigotry and narrowness in the guise of science and objective truth.

Two examples suffice. When I was an undergraduate, the theory of continental drift was condemned and ridiculed as impossible, there not being a shred of evidence for its occurrence. Now, continental drift is a litmus test of the true scientific mind, and only those impervious to knowledge do not believe in it, according to the establishment. The other example is the question of whether the universe is finite or infinite. Scientific dogma has changed on this over the years, yet one side or the other of this unprovable and essentially religious question has been insisted upon as an established fact.

[July, 1990; age 39]

1215. A way of looking is also a way of not looking.
— Chinese Proverb

1216. From *The Book of One Hundred Lies*:
  32. "You'll have an opportunity to approve any decision we make about this before it's put into effect." or "We won't do an-

ything without asking you first."

[May 1991; age 40]

1217. Do not hang your head and gloomily resign yourself to God's will; rather seek his will with joy and strive to perform it with confidence and enthusiasm.

1218. Problems arrive in fast cars, but they leave on foot.

1219. Good looks deserve high praise; good works deserve higher praise.

1220. Do not tie your shoe in a strawberry patch. [After the Chinese proverb, "In a field of melons, do not pull up your shoe; under a plum tree, do not adjust your cap." Don't engage in behavior that can be easily misinterpreted.]

[July, 1991; age 40]

1221. Most people are not reasoned into faith but faith must be reasonable—make sense—have the support of the intellect—or it will not be lasting and effective. The heart and the mind talk with each other and strive to be in harmony. When they are not, an impossible tension results.

1222. The angrier someone gets when you disagree with him, the less certain he is that he is right. See Pascal's headache in the *Pensees*.

1223. Real change takes a long time, but not always.

1224. Bad experiences make good stories.

1225. It's not just the events themselves but the assumptions you have about the events that control the way you respond to the events.

1226. Three purposes of education: (1) to gain knowledge of how life works: *dulce et utile*; (2) to learn how to apply knowledge appropriately, make good decisions, solve problems; (3) to understand the paradoxes of life and human nature, gain wisdom.

1227. There is a difference between reading a book and engaging a text. Engagement comes in thinking along with the author, sometimes arguing with him, sometimes suspending judgment, never allowing ourselves to stuff him into one of our intellectual file folders, labeled with some sweeping generalization. "That book? Oh, yeah, I read it. He says that we only think we are happy." "The Bible? Yeah, it's about self improvement."

1228. Time is a factor we often neglect in the cleaning process. Many stains cannot be just washed out; many accretions cannot be just rinsed off. Either prolonged scrubbing, or more commonly, some soaking, is needed. The same is true with stains of the heart. Time is needed to dissolve them.

[December, 1991; age 41]

1229. Consistency over time is better than a single amazement. A small candle lit constantly is of more value than the brilliant flash of a meteor. We are dazzled by momentary brilliance, but we live with constancy. Men love by suddenness, women by accretion.

1230. One of the great sayings of ancient philosophy is "Know thyself." Self knowledge is the basis for sanity and coherent action. Another saying should be added to this: "Know others." By understanding other people we become compassionate and tolerant and forgiving.

1231. Our souls are unique, but our lives—our experiences, actions, and decisions—are not, just as a given doll is unique, though her body, clothes, and range of movement are common to all the other dolls of the same type. It is offensive to our pride to think of ourselves as types, yet in some respects that is the case.

1232. Just having someone for company, sitting nearby, is a blessing and an enjoyment, something many people do not realize. You can see true friends sitting near each other on the grass, each reading silently or doing homework. Others say, "If you're not doing something together, why be together?" They don't understand.

1233. What I liked about T—: She had a sprightly personality and was really cute, but I liked her loving heart. She was determined to be kind to others. Several times during the semester she hugged me with enthusiasm, with a real hug—not with one of those shoulder-blade-only imitation hugs. It's rejuvenating to hug a beautiful girl, to feel her head against my head, and her body against mine.

I also liked T—'s sweet-but-determined-and-matter-of-fact way she approached little problems. A couple of times during the semester, she noticed on the grade sheet that the grades for an assignment were missing or that she had been marked absent when she wasn't. She would say something like, "Well, we've got to clear this up right away," in a tone that I can't really describe—not at all threatening or aggressive or blame casting, but in the same tone one might say, "I need to buy another pencil," only with something about it that is amusing in a nice way.

Speaking of amusing, one day I said to her, "You look sweet today," and she looked at me for perhaps fifteen seconds with an odd expression, as if she couldn't figure out what to say. Finally she said, "I am" in a mildly childlike way. I laughed. Anyway, she was a teddy bear in fox's clothing. My hug therapist.

Unfortunately, when the semester ended, she stopped acting so friendly, as a lot of female students do.

1234. What I liked about R—: I was going to say that R— treated me with respect, but that sounds too formal, and implies an inequality that I don't mean to. I think the best way of putting it is to say that R— was unassuming and not presumptuous. For example, one day she came into my office with a headache. She didn't ask for some aspirin. I offered it to her. Then I took out a little bottle of water from my refrigerator and handed it to her. She said something like, "That's neat," and then, "Can I keep this?" with a tone of doubt or surprise or incredulity. So of course I said, "No, R—, now that I've shown it to you, give it back." She was very grateful for a 30-cent bottle of water. Contrast that with a couple of other students who not only come into my office and ask for water or juice without hesitation (which is fine—that's why I stock the stuff) but who, when I'm not there, come in and help themselves. I'm not implying that the help-themselves people are wrong in any way, for they are welcome to the stuff. It's just that R—'s attitude was somehow so nice (again I was going to say respectful but didn't).

The first time I asked R— out to lunch (on the phone it was) she said, "I'd *love* to have lunch with you." That enthusiasm really touched me. A lot of girls say yes reluctantly or so deliberately that I feel like they'd rather not, but will under pressure.

1235. What I liked about S—: She actually *read* Marcus Aurelius when I gave her a copy. She also wrote out quotations from him and put them up at her desk where she could read them. I found this all out when I visited D— and S— one open house night in order to install a shower head for them.

S— was also really cute—one day in the dining commons she was the only girl at the table with seven guys sitting around her, talking long after their food was gone—yet she was humble.

1236. Things you can't say. While thinking about different people for the "What I like about X" notes I was making above, it once again occurred to me that there are some things one cannot say. For example, it's okay for me to tell a girl that I like her hair, but it would be considered inappropriate for me to remark about some other body parts. I first realized this more than fifteen years ago when I was at a mall, where I saw a girl with the most kissable lips I have ever seen. Something about them just looked inviting. She was with a guy, but even if she had been by herself I couldn't very well have walked up and told her what I thought. That would sound like such a line.

Much more recently, one of my students wore short shorts to class almost every day, and was in the habit of propping her feet up on the desk in front of her, thus putting her legs on display. Even though she has nice legs, I couldn't very well tell her, "I enjoyed your legs this semester," or even "You have nice legs." The professor is not supposed to notice, so if anyone asks, I didn't see a thing.

(I was encouraged to write down these last Glimmerings by reading in *The Pillow Book of Sei Shonagon*. I thought some comments and vignettes like this might not be bad, even though they are not strictly philosophical.)

1237. What I liked about L—: She was another of those girls who understands the enjoyment of simple fellowship. When she was in a class that met at my house, she would sometimes stay after just to spend time with me—for no "reason," with no topic to discuss, no agenda to advance. Some subject (or usually several) would come up. I really enjoyed those times. She wouldn't even complain about the coldness of her boyfriend (as another girl does every time I see her) unless I raised the subject. (I've known her through three or four boyfriends now.)

Several weeks ago she came over to clean and instead we spent the time just talking in front of the fire. (She drove about 20 miles each way at night to do this.) A year or so back she used to clean in the afternoon and I'd get home to find a pot of coffee waiting. (I used to open the door and say, "Hi, dear, I'm home," and she'd say, "So how was work today?") When she was finished with the house, she'd stay a good while and talk. I miss those "old days"!

She also did an excellent job cleaning my house—above and

beyond the call of duty, I'd say. And when I forgot she was coming and the check wasn't there when she came (and I was at school), she didn't even mention it, even though she was desperate for cash. I'll bet she would have cleaned free (at least once) if I had asked her to. Just for the sake of completeness in this larcenous age, I should mention that L— is honest — messy guy that I am, I leave money on my dresser and sometimes lying around downstairs or on my desk, and she never took anything. The fact that she came from a wild and worldly background is testimony to the power of the Lord.

1238. What I like about my mom: In one word, it's "supportive." When I'm at her house, whenever I start doing something outside, she will come around and offer to help. If I'm trimming branches or grass or washing my car, she will jump right in and help. But it's the encouragement that's really important, the moral support. For example, if I'm working on my car, say changing the oil or doing a repair, she will come down to the garage and ask how she can help. She will offer to get tools, bring me water or coffee, or anything to show her support, even though she can't help on the repair itself. I remember one of my old Glimmerings, something like, "He who holds the tools is as valuable as he who uses them."

If I say I want to do something, go somewhere, even buy something, she's in favor of it, even willing to help pay for it.

1239. My reading in the *Pillow Book* (see Glimmering #1236) has also interested me in writing some simple, almost Japanese-style poetry. Here's a poem I wrote to give to a friend:

When the sun glides beyond the mountains
And takes the day to another place,
I think of you.

The literal meaning is that when the busy day is over and darkness comes, I think about her. The metaphorical meaning is that when she, sunshine person that she is, goes away, I think about her. Of course there is the implication of a bit of lonesomeness, too. This poem I was going to print on stiff, textured paper with a rough right edge lined with red or green marker. I was going to attach a sprig of redwood tree to it (suggesting the mountains left behind by the sun).

1240. What I liked about S—: A few years ago I had a girlfriend named S—. We soon discovered that we were from different planets, but we had a few months of enjoyment. She was smart, a good writer, playful, and sometimes affectionate. What I enjoyed most, I think, was cuddling up with her in front of the fire on a rainy Sunday afternoon, just listening to the rain. I liked nuzzling her hair and just holding her as we half dozed. Some people like—or even demand—thrills every minute, but just getting together to be together is enjoyable to me.

Sometimes she would come over after work at about 10:00 pm too tired to do anything, but she came over anyway and we would just talk or cuddle or lie in front of the fire and listen to classical music. (She liked rock music, but she also liked classical a bit and I find rock irritating.)

I read once that a famous model, Paulina I think, said that she really liked just making popcorn and watching TV with her boyfriend. Simple times can be the best times.

1241. What I liked about D—: Back in graduate school days, I pursued a girl named D—. One thing that still stands out to me happened one evening when she invited me over for dinner. I was watching the news while she prepared dinner and she brought me a cup of hot tea. That may seem like a small gesture, but it was a powerful symbol of kindness and affection, and I remember it a dozen years later (and have remembered it a number of times before now). Ten years after that event, another young lady and I were sitting around together when she got up, got herself a glass of milk, came back and sat down. She didn't ask me if I wanted some milk or a more general, "Do you want anything?" or "Can I get you something while I'm up?"

Again, no big deal, I suppose, but it's the kind of thing one re-members—and makes generalizations about, whether rightly or wrongly.

[January 1, 1992; age 41]

1242. Culture is a constantly developing set of values and prac-tices that can be adopted or selected eclectically by anyone. Ide-ally culture should be dynamic, seeking unceasingly the best ways to solve social problems and enhance the lives of a given society.

1243. Of course the machinery is important, but take the time to attend to the oil that lubricates the machinery.

1244. All judgment is by comparison: it follows that the more things you know about, the better your judgment can become because you will have more things to compare. Thus the bene-fits of travel and reading.

1245. **Lessons from Housekeeping #1**.
A major component in the cleaning process is time. Adver-tisers try to sell products under the implication that no time is necessary: "Just spray it on and wipe it off." If you're just dust-ing, that's fine. But with real dirt only by letting a minute or five pass can the cleaners really work. The dirt requires time to dis-solve and loosen, and degreasers need time to break down and liquefy the grease.

This is just one more lesson from the natural world about the importance of patience, brought to you by the Creator of the natural world, who wants us to learn patience. No wonder we are so interested in immediate gratification, since we always seem to be pulled in directions opposite to those we should be.

Time is also required on the human level for cleaning the dirt out of our souls. Once we cease to swim in the septic tanks of life, time must pass before we feel fully clean emotionally and spiritually.

1246. Somewhere in another work is a list of top ten books, but here is one more try. Okay, you are going to be stuck on a desert island for your obvious crimes against society, and you can take any ten books you want with you. They must be actually existing books. (Next time I do this, I might cheat and let myself take CD ROM's like the 240-volume world literature library, etc. etc. Not this time.)

So here they are:

1. The Bible, NASB translation. Even though I've been reading in the NIV most recently, I'd probably take my well-underlined NASB.

2. Thomas a Kempis, *The Imitation of Christ* in the Richard Whitford translation. There are a number of things to be critical about in Thomas' book, but there are many really good passages.

3. Marcus Aurelius, *Meditations.* The comment about Thomas applies here, too. Marcus even alludes to suicide a few times, but on the whole, this is a really good book for shaking the cobwebs out of the head and clearing the pettiness out of the heart.

4. Samuel Johnson, *Rasselas.* One of my favorite books. Short for a desert island, but I'll take it anyway.

5. *The Air Force Survival Manual.* I hope I can take some tools, too, like a knife and a hatchet.

6. The *Random House Encyclopedia.* This one-volume monster has lots of color pictures and interesting articles that would keep me busy on rainy days. It also describes how to build roads and bridges, etc.

7. A one-volume poetry and prose of John Milton, I think.

8. George Herbert's *Works* in the Oxford English Texts edition.

9. and 10. This gets difficult. I'd like to take Boswell's *Life of Johnson,* but I'd really like to take Johnson's *Ramblers,* but they are in three volumes. Shakespeare would be okay as would a Bible commentary, maybe. I do have a collected dialogues of Plato volume, but I'm not sure I'd reach for it first. There are

many good books, Plato, Aristotle, Cicero, but what are the ten at the very top? Maybe Pascal's *Pensees* should go along. Or a book of proverbs. Or maybe *The Dictionary of Thoughts*, a quotation dictionary. Yes, that would be number 9. I do have a Johnson collection that includes *Rasselas*, so I'll take that as #4 and get a few *Ramblers* and other stuff as well. Well, for now, let's say Boswell for #10.

1247. Heraclitus says that men's eyes and ears will deceive them if their souls lack understanding (*On the Universe,* IV). If a man's soul is mud, he will see mud, though he look upon a snowflake. Sight and experience are not in themselves truth; the proper understanding of what one sees and experiences is truth.

1248. Heraclitus also says that seeking the unexpected is difficult (*On the Universe,* VII). Here is an affirmation of the value of imagination.

1249. **A couple of comments from reading Marcus Aurelius again:**

III.7 Do not pursue anything that will cost you your integrity (even if you are the only person who will know it). A small lie will cost your sense of self more than the value the lie will purchase. If you cannot ask openly for what you want, or get what you want openly, then your goal is incompatible with the health of your soul.

IV.3 "Things can never touch the soul," and "Life itself is but what you deem it." It is not the events themselves but how you respond to them that determines what they are. Some people constantly victimize themselves by receiving every small unpleasantness as a crisis, while others see even major difficulties as challenges for them to show what they are made of. Thus, some people seem always to be in a hysterical fit of panic, while others seem to have few problems.

IV.36 There is no final product: everything is the seed of something else.

IV.44 "Everything that happens is as normal and expected

as the spring rose or the summer fruit." Samuel Johnson once said that "a wise man is never surprised." Isn't it odd how many people run around in a constant state of disbelief about rather simple events: "I can't believe he said that"; "I can't see how anyone could believe that"; "I can't believe they would do that." And so on. Shouldn't we expect things outside of our own experience to be possible?

VI.10 Here is the basic key to human behavior and values. All actions and values derive from a belief about purpose. If I have a rock in one hand and a watch in the other, I cannot say which is more useful until I describe the purpose I have in mind. If my intent (purpose) is to tell time, the watch is more useful. If my intent is to provide a sunning spot for my frog, the rock is more useful. Similarly, until we know the purpose of human life, we can make no conclusions about what is good or bad in life. Albert Camus, the French existentialist, decided that life had no purpose, so that the only important question was whether or not to kill yourself — pretty much as Marcus predicted such a person would think.

1250. The strangest thing about women is their masochism; the strangest thing about men is their egg-shell egos.

1251. Three things we need to improve our society and our world: (1) good ideas, (2) the design of effective systems, and (3) a recapturing of values (love, charity, duty, fellowship, respect, generosity, honesty, etc.). Actually, (1) and (2) are probably the same. I am ever more convinced of the importance of ideas — new ways of doing things or solving problems. We tend too much to grind away at problems with solutions that really don't work. We need effort and commitment, of course, but we really need that new idea that will help us solve the problem better, faster, with less cost or fewer drawbacks.

Yet how little respect and time are devoted to ideas — to thinking, or imagining possibilities, to playing with solutions.

1252. No, Glimmering #1250 is not right. The strangest thing about women is their capacity for self-deception; the strangest thing about men is the criteria they use to measure themselves and other people.

1253. I recently found a notebook taken with me on a trip to England and Ireland in 1977. Here are the thoughts extracted from it:

If you wonder why the world is messed up, just listen to someone recount to a third party some information you've both heard: the recount is wrong, mixed up, etc.

Overheard: "She must be an Irish tinker's daughter — she can't stay in one place for five minutes."

Give a man a sack of cement powder and you've given him a house. [The idea being that he can find sand and rocks and water anywhere to combine with the cement.]

"It's got to be English money; we've no use for anything else." — Newspaper lady in Scotland

The Clydesdale bank has three closed circuit TV monitors in the front window showing the safe fronts and the cash windows.

Epitaphs in a Scotch cemetery:

All you that come my grave to see,
prepare my friends to follow me,
repent in time make no delay,
for I in haste was call'd away.

Stop now and cast an eye
as you are now so once were we,
as we are now so must you be,
short was our lives
long be our rest,
Christ took us home
when he thought best.

Sign in a garden:

The kiss of the sun for pardon
The song of the birds for mirth
One is nearer God's heart in a garden
Than anywhere else on earth.

Sign: "The use of cooking appliances using a naked flame is prohibited."

Note etched in concrete around a culvert cover: "Rome wasn't built in a day; this was."

The sea is saying, "I am patient and I will persevere, and I will win."

Rich books, rich dreams.

Most people who want to be livers act like spleens.

People who butt in front of you in line are one thing, but unwashed people who butt in are another altogether.

Overheard at a London Cabaret: "What do you think of the show so far?" "Rubbish."

1254. The first law of sociology is that people shape each other. One culture influences another, our society influences us as individuals, and our friends, spouse, parents, children — all help shape our attitudes, values, thinking, and behaviors.

Thus, we should choose our friends, and especially our spouse, well aware that these people will have a profound influence on the core of our being. I doubt that, when we are thinking about whether or not we want to marry someone, we ever stop to ask, "Is this the person I want to be shaped by? Are these the personality traits and values and thinking habits that I want to be a significant influence on my soul?" (And, of course, there is the less selfish question, "Is this the person I want to have an influence on my children as we raise them together?" And maybe another unselfish question is, "Is this the person I want to shape, a person who will be improved by my influence rather than hurt or made worse?")

1255. Maturity is the process of exchanging your anti-social ego defense mechanisms for socially positive ones.

1256. "Hi, Sir, this is Annie with Shy Steer Resorts. Congratulations! You have won one of six prizes with no obligation to buy anything!"

"Thank you, but my life is already too glutted with possessions that I have no time to enjoy. Perhaps someone else will respond to your offer in the way it deserves."

1257. No, Glimmering #1252 is not right. The strangest thing about women is that they expect men to be mind readers. ("If he loved me, he would know how I feel, what I'm thinking, and what I want.") The strangest thing about men is that they will lie to women without any apparent motivation.

1258. Heraclitus says that "the sun is new every day" (*On the Universe*, XXXII) and that "you cannot step into the same river twice" (XLI and LXXXI). This must therefore mean that we never speak to the same person twice, for the friend we meet again is always a little different, having grown or at least changed. Let us remember this, and not demand that people stop their development just to please us. Let us realize that attitudes and beliefs change and that our pigeon holes are not really adequate for putting those we love—or hate—into.

1259. We are not put on earth just to consume resources and add to the global waste stream. Each of us has a duty to contribute something to the advancement of civilization.

1260. The world runs on ideas. Not on oil, computer power, or wheels, but on ideas. I'd like to say, "The world runs on good ideas," but sometimes it runs on bad ones, because good ones are scarce. There are two kinds of ideas. First are the ideas of values—what we call wisdom—ideas that tell us what human nature is like, what the Good is, why we should act, who we are, and so forth. The second are the ideas that solve problems and enhance our lives. Perhaps we could call these two categories the philosophical and the technical.

1261. Re the fire and brimstone sermons that were once popular. Do we really need the thought of God glowering at us or being enraged at us before we will find motivation to serve him? Just think how you would feel if, when you get to heaven, instead of, "Well done, good and faithful servant," God says, "Oh, it's you." Isn't *that* thought sufficient to motivate you? Fearing just the tsk of God should be enough to spur us to activity and goodness.

1262. Three couplets found among my early writings:

> Like damps unknown condensed within the heart
> That linger there and rust the soul apart.

> Let not your doubts a hidden bane be proved,
> Or 'gainst yourself, yourself be moved.

> So is that fear which rises out of doubt
> And stays to see the shaken mind cast out.

1263. Craftsmen sometimes view the work of their competitors very critically. Bring a painter out to your house and he says, "It looks like the last guy who painted this was an amateur." Your new auto mechanic says, "I can't believe they get money for doing work like this."

Did you ever wonder whether the people who work on *you* have the same thoughts—only they don't express them, of course. Your new dentist looks into your mouth and thinks, "Who put this junk into your mouth? I've never seen somebody take so many shortcuts." The only hint you get of his thinking is an odd question, "Do you like to take long vacations in third world countries?" Next day your new doctor examines you, noting your surgical scar. "Did you pay for this butchery?" he thinks to himself. "That's the shape of scar made by those fossilized dumbos who still use the Smervits technique. Who licenses these quacks anyway?"

1264. We spend too much time trying to orchestrate serendipity.

1265. And did you think that love has no price?

1266. As much as we talk about the value of planning and the lessons of experience, we still seem to live most of our lives ad hoc.

1267. If marriage is a state of perpetual friendship, a mutual exchange of affection, an affiliation for regular sex, a relationship of shared intimacy, then it follows that marriage is not a discreet state, but a confederation that admits of degrees. Thus, we should not ask simply, "Do you want to get married?" but, "How married do you want to be?" For some people want to be more married than others.

1268. History is an interpretation of selected events a historian has judged to be important from among those he believes to have taken place.

1269. What I liked about D—. A few years ago I sold my old car to D—. It needed some fixing up so I agreed to do the work. In order to repair the brake system, I had to get on the floor under the dash. When I squirmed onto my back to squeeze under there, I was surprised to see that D— immediately—instantly—turned over onto her back and slid down next to me to help. Not many girls, it seems to me, are (1) willing to put themselves into awkward postures for any reason and (2) get dirty with real dirt—grease, etc. and (3) help do something mechanical. D— literally dove into this job, doing all these things at once. True, it was her car, but I was impressed anyway.

1270. Our ideas about perfection are drawn improperly from certain technological metaphors. In some technologies, there is only one perfect, and everything else deviates. With human beings, however, perfect is often a range or even a category rather than a single point or summit. Several shapes of nose may be described as "perfect," for example. So we could say of two people, considering their words, personalities, physical characteristics, etc., "They are both perfect and both different."

1271. You think the other person is listening to your answer to some question, but in reality the other person is really studying you—are you a model? Is your behavior worthy of imitation? Did the question upset you and should it have? Should I be upset, too? One of the unnerving truths about teaching is that the things we pronounce with importance are ignored and our offhand comments are woven into our hearers' souls.

1272. Men like dogs, because dogs can be dominated, ordered around, and loved whenever their master feels like it. But women are like cats, who cannot be dominated or ordered around, and who must be loved on their own terms when they feel like it. This means trouble in paradise.

1273. Exodus 34. We've got to make the tablets before God will write on them. He wants us to do our part and not sit back and expect him to do everything.

1274. The more you admit your abnormalities to others, the more normal you make them feel. If you admit that you sometimes get depressed, or feel lonely, or say stupid things, you will make your hearers feel more fully human as they realize that their shortcomings and failures are the common lot of mankind and not some perverted aberration unique to themselves. People are conformists because they want to feel normal.

1275. When you know that you know nothing, you know much.

1276. Believing an incorrect clock produces an optical delusion.

1277. We are all very principled and philosophical until a tragedy or an opportunity arrives and then we follow our emotions.

1278. A bird is overjoyed to chomp down a bug or a worm.

1279. The successful in romance, career, and problem solving are the ones who "perform reality" and do not insist on doing things strictly according to theory or idealized scripts or with baseless prejudices. The socially or romantically popular script for meeting a girl and "falling in love" or proposing marriage is quite different from what most often takes place in the actual world. Life cannot be lived by recipe.

1280. From a note written in the darkness in the middle of the night when half asleep (meaning that it may be meaningless or even brilliant): "Pilot logic, associative logic, dialog logic: three uses for an outline to develop each of these. Associative logic = analogy and organization." (This Glimmering is a reminder to transcribe notes as soon as possible before I forget what they mean.)

1281. Beauty does not happen fast. All acts of beauty happen slowly — writing poetry, painting a picture, singing a hymn.

1282. Most people who have messed up their lives want happiness without having to change their values.

1283. Some see the goal but not the path; others see the path but not the goal. The former must learn to risk; the latter must learn to trust.

1284. Are belief structures a political act? That is, since I'm rejected by or since I reject the "establishment," I believe in UFO's, astrology, pyramid power, etc. Or, because I hate authority or reject my father's cruel parenting, I'm an atheist, an anarchist, etc. Are beliefs emotional and political responses as well as intellectual ones?

1285. How does a resident of Murzuk or Adrar or Bilma or Ati

differ in outlook from us? Is his vision limited? Does he see
fewer things as being possible? We make choices not from what
is possible but from what we believe is possible. So education is
a process of unfolding the realm of the possible.

1286. A narrow minded poverty of imagination, a lack of empathy, makes people selfish and inflexible, prisoners of a single
view, a one-dimensional life. The cure: To be able to see a situation or all of life from alternate viewpoints, from the viewpoints
of other people, to be circumspect, to flex the imagination—and
the heart.

1287. How fascinating that we manage to adapt our basic discontent to any level or lifestyle. Now in the middle class we
have hot and cold running water, indoor flush toilets, stereos,
aspirin, air transport, washers and dryers, automatic forced air
heating and cooling—things even kings did not have a couple
of hundred years ago—yet we are no more content than the
people then. Maybe we are less so because we have been taught
to expect more.

1288. Modern marriages are less happy than older ones because
the distance between expectation and reality has been increased.
For some reason, many people expect that marriage will solve
all of their problems and be uninterrupted blazing hilarity. I
hope I am reading this.

1289. Is art the expression of experience, the preservation of experience, or should it be virtual experience?

1290. When we teach, we should teach (1) information, (2) the
significance or importance of the information, (3) the implications of the information for personal life (seeking changes, making decisions), and (4) the effect the information has on the
learning process (how does it help teach analysis, create inductive conclusions, making judgments, conceptualizing).

1291. Wisdom and virtue come in the exchange, transmission and enunciation of values. Speak your proverbs often and they will change the world. Live your proverbs and you will change the world.

1292. There are worse things than being fired and worse things than death. These two facts you must know in order to lead a moral life.

1293. Modern art and culture: Landfill on display, garage sale leftovers, guardians of the wastebasket, visual noise, the harbinger of neobarbarism, grandma's trash can.

1294. Question your doubts. —Proverb.

1295. Trust is the very first stone in the foundation of any relationship. It is the same whether a personal relationship, a business relationship, or a relationship with God.

1296. Take time to observe and to share.

1297. What makes a person lovable, a real friend, is not his being always right or wholly agreeable but his being genuine and honest about his beliefs. Those who hesitate to say what they really think or who vacillate keep us from loving them as real friends. They don't seem to trust us enough to reveal themselves and we in turn find it difficult to trust them enough to be their friends. True friends should let each other know what each really believes.

1298. In our society the fake gets higher billing than the real, the appearance is promoted over the reality. The actress whose face plays the part gets big billing, but the dancer whose body really does all the work for the actress is almost ignored. The same is true with the stunt stand ins, the special effects people, all those who make the appearance of film happen. Real life is similar: the secretaries who make life happen get much lower billing than the executives.

1299. Painful Truth Department: "Tell me, Chamberlain, what do my subjects think of me?" "Truly, Sire, your subjects despise you in their hearts and would gladly see your bloated and rotting carcass being eaten by scab-covered vultures on a fly-blown desert plain."

1300. Why does your brain always have to say, "Let's get realistic," when your heart wants to fly?

1301. Isn't it amazing how often part of our prayer to God is, "Thank you for not laughing"?

1302. We try to live our lives in an orderly and consistent way by using generalizations. But in the application of our beliefs, we often change our generalizations to allow for persuasive exceptions. For example, we think, "I'd never marry a girl with purple hair," and as long as we never meet such a girl, our generalization is fine. We even reject a date with a girl said to have purple hair based on this generalization. But then one day we meet a wonderful girl—witty, laughing, attractive, fun, smart—with purple hair—and we discover that we cannot remember why we were living our lives by such a generalization.

What we should do, then, is to be cautious of generalizations that are really unexamined prejudices.

1303. Don't worry if other people seem to be confident when you are feeling nervous and uncertain. They are living their lives for the first time, too, and are probably less confident than you think.

1304. A Proverb improved: Give a man a fish and he will have a meal; teach a man how to fish and he will have many meals; teach a man how to think about how to fish and he will feed the world.

1305. If wishes were kisses, we'd all be covered with slobber.
— Ancient Dendrite Proverb

1306. There is a great difference between being blessed and recognizing that we are blessed. Many times we mistake a blessing for a lack of blessing or even for harm.

1307. The bipolar model of human life is often incorrect. We cannot say that we are either happy or unhappy, because we are both. Similarly, to the question, Does love make life more simple or more complex, the answer is, Both. Life becomes more simple and more complex at the same time.

1308. The first time he kissed her he said, "That's about as close to virtual reality as you can get without a computer."

1309. Too many people in romantic relationships don't love each other; too many people who *are* in love are not friends.

1310. Love is the most serious thing in the world, which is all the more reason it ought to be fun.

1311. Does God love you any less when your lover dumps you than when you meet a new and wonderful love? No. Why then do you whine and doubt at the former and give thanks only at the latter?

1312. Much of the damage we do to ourselves comes from trying to take shortcuts to happiness.

1313. The strangest thing about women is that they think they can change their husbands; the strangest thing about men is that they think their wives will never change.

1314. The trouble with too many Christian guys is that they want to be obedient to Christ until they stretch out on the floor next to a nice girl.

1315. It's good not to be materialistic, not to see objects like pens and clocks and art objects as possessing extreme value. But perhaps it is good not to see some things as just objects, either. To see a favorite pen, for example, not as just any pen but as a friend, as something one has some attachment to, maybe that isn't all bad. When someone's house burns down, he is much less attached to any objects, and we usually describe that fact as a good thing. But maybe a respect for or even a joy in some simple things (pens, calculators, stuffed animals) is really a good thing, too.

1316. "What makes a man love a woman is simple and straightforward; what makes a woman love a man is the mystery of the ages." —Proverb

But what is simple about a man's love? Is it that he loves a woman for her body, or her attractiveness, or her personality, or all three? And do all men love for the same reason? And do all women love for the same reason or in the same way?

1317. Two important lessons for men to learn about women: (1) When a woman gets cranky and frustrated, she is not necessarily cranky and frustrated because of you. (2) When a woman gets cranky and frustrated with you, she doesn't necessarily love you any less. In fact, be understanding and she'll love you even more—when she recovers her mood.

1318. What are the big lessons God wants us to learn in our lives here on earth? I think they are these:

(1) **Trust him.** We have a tendency to rely on ourselves or on others or on money, our position of power, etc. to control events as we would have them instead of realizing that God knows what's best for us.

(2) **Be patient.** For some reason, this is a lesson we need to be taught over and over. Why we are supposed to learn to be patient, I don't know, but it certainly is a big one on God's list.

(3) **Love others.** It may seem odd that we should need to

learn how to love, but we all could use improvement. We need to love selflessly, not with an idea of getting something for our effort. We need to learn the love of (a) giving to others and (b) being compassionate and understanding, not so critical and judgmental of every thing and person we don't understand.

1319. Communication too often seems to break down or be imperfect in romantic relationships. To prevent this from happening, I suggest that multiple channels of communication be implemented, so that when one doesn't work, another will. Here are some possible channels:

1. Talk.

2. Write letters and notes.

3. Give or play a song with meaningful lyrics that convey your feelings.

4. Call and talk on the phone.

5. Write a poem.

6. Give a poem or story or book with a meaning you want to convey.

7. Give a symbolic gift—flowers, a stuffed animal, jewelry, perfume.

8. Give a cartoon revealing human nature or some appropriate message.

9. Caress each other silently. Stroke an arm, back. Nuzzle hair.

10. Read together. The Bible, an article, a book with a message you would like to communicate.

11. See a movie together that opens an issue you want to discuss.

12. Write a story that conveys your feelings.

1320. Just because you love each other doesn't mean you should get married. If you aren't compatible, you might find yourself saying, "I love you too much to marry you." If the love is real, such a sentence could make sense.

1321. It's easier to add love to friendship than friendship to love.

It's easier to add pleasure to love than love to pleasure. The trouble with many relationships is that they start backward. They start with pleasure (physical attraction, kissing) and then add or try to add love. Later, if the relationship continues, the couple may try to add friendship. This is very difficult. But if you begin with friendship, then add love, then add pleasure, you will most likely have a fun and lasting relationship.

1322. Their love began with only a spark of kindness, just bright enough to ignite an ember of interest into a gentle glow. The breath of friendship, exhaling across these warming coals, then puffed them into the flame of love, which burned ever more brightly until finally it rose to incandescence and illuminated their very souls with joy.

1323. Our formal education usually involves the learning of generalizations and guidelines, whether for technical applications or for life. After we have learned a quantity of these, we sometimes tend to be cocky and think we know the secrets of the universe. But after our formal schooling, in the actual application of our knowledge, our experience teaches us the exceptions and the refinements without which our knowledge is imperfect, and our generalizations are too sweeping or inaccurate. As the matrix of exceptions and refinements grows more complex, we become more careful and more humble.

1324. We are often motivated to move closer to God in times of stress and unhappiness and crisis, for then we recognize that we truly need him for help and even daily existence. We are similarly motivated to move closer to him in times of great happiness and success, for our gratitude at his goodness and generosity, especially in the face of our clear lack of desert, overwhelms us with feelings of love and thanksgiving. But it is also important to love God in the ordinary times, to find the motivation to move closer to him when things are operating in routine mode, in second gear, in normal haze, on a typical day. For God's consistent and regular love, his long term sustenance in our routine lives, is no less great and amazing than what he does for us in moments of defeat or of triumph.

1325. **Lessons Learned from the Los Angeles Riots, 1992.**

1. The thin veneer of civilization is really much thinner than we are willing to believe. Police, fire, and ambulance services have too few resources and too little power to maintain control or safety if even a modest number of people decide to get out of control. Only a consensus of self control keeps civilization working.

2. Many people do not live thoughtful lives; they simply react opportunistically and selfishly, doing whatever they think they can get away with. A philosophical sense of morality, or acting on the basis of a moral code, seems to be a lost art.

3. Technology is only a tool—it is not civilization. A can of gasoline can be used equally as a tool of advancement (in a car) or as a weapon (in a gasoline bomb). A van can be used to heal (as an ambulance) or to harm (as a means of hauling away booty from looting a store).

1326. It's too bad that we have such a resistant attitude toward suffering. I've learned a lot from suffering—from loneliness, rejection, unrequited love, grief, physical pain, and occasionally fear, anxiety, and worry. We indeed grow more contemplative and introspective in such times; we think about what's really important, where our anchor really is, what the true center of our lives and souls really is. And if we are wise, we reconfirm that only God can be counted on to be our friend, our anchor, our pivot. Suffering makes us both more philosophical and wise and more faithful.

1327. When we tell someone, "You're on the wrong path," we expect instant change: "Oh? Okay, I'll change my life and behavior completely right now." But no one responds this way. Instead people say, "What do you mean I'm on the wrong path? No, I'm not. So just shut up and leave me alone." We leave, discouraged and convinced that our attempt at help was worthless just because we didn't see instant change. (We want instant everything these days.) And yet our words will work in the hearts of those we admonish; it may take days, weeks, months, or even years, because change is often slow. So we should continue to talk and to realize the value of it.

1328. Does the sun envy the rain because the rain gives moisture to the soil and the juice of life to every plant? Does the wind envy the stars because they show the vastness of the universe and remind us that not even darkness is without hopeful light? No, all things in the natural world perform their appointed function without regret or envy. Can we do less, we who are chosen and loved by God? [inspired by Marcus Aurelius, 6.43]

1329. Two things we neglect:
    1. The record of your life is permanent. Every act, every word will last forever. Nothing is ever lost or forgotten.
    2. We get only one pass through life. We don't get a trial run, a second trip, another chance now that we have learned by our follies. The first time is the only time.

1330. It's said, "Forgive and forget," "Kiss and make up," and so on after hard words. But hard words — cruel words — are never erased. "Healing" will take place to some extent, but emotional scars will always be there. Once you call your husband or wife or son or daughter a jerk, an idiot, an insensitive fool, or just yell in anger, your relationship will be changed — lessened — forever. That's why so few people are really close and warm after a long marriage. Think a long time, then, before you lash out. Remember the proverbs: "A word, once spoken, can never be recalled" and "The blow from an angry word can hurt for years."

1331. You want to live longer? You want to live a long time? And what have you done with the time you've had so far? Didn't waste any? Used it so well that more would be good? Or did you waste a lot of it in foolishness and now you want more to make up for the way you squandered the previous allotment? Would you use the extra time for good or to increase your personal quantity of sin and idiocy and idle self-indulgence?

1332. Civilization is an incremental process, so every good idea, however small, is valuable.

1333. Your purpose, your job, on this earth is to serve God — to help his creatures (and to prepare your own soul). There are some things about this you do not know and some things that others could help you with. Why then are you hesitant to admit ignorance or to ask for help? It would be silly to allow your pride to interfere with your purpose for existence, to hinder the very job you are here to do. Be frank and forthright therefore in asking for what you need; shame or coyness would be ridiculous. [inspired by Marcus Aurelius, 7.7]

1334. Thinking of the previous Glimmering: What is it that makes us unwilling to state frankly what we are thinking, feeling, wanting, or needing? Is it embarrassment? Fear? Shame? What is there for "so little a creature as man" to be embarrassed about? And what is this fear — that you will die? Or just be laughed at? And shame — the fear that you are not measuring up — to what or whom? Let us therefore resolve to be forthright and, as long as we are not insulting or hurting others, say what is on our minds, whether to admit ignorance, express uneasiness, or whatever it is that we normally suppress out of too much concern for ourselves and "what people will think" about us.

1335. You say you are worried because you do not know the future. Does this mean that you have lived so thoroughly and effectively today that you now have time left over to live in the future? Shouldn't you instead worry about finishing today first?

1336. "Your every separate action should contribute towards an integrated life." — Marcus Aurelius, 8.32

A life that is well focused and well ordered will reflect or embody or be possessed of integration—a coherence and a wholeness. Your life should have a clarifying and centering goal, around which you can construct all your activities.

1337. Sweets for the sweet, nuts for the nutty, pretzels for the twisted.

1338. Strive to keep your soul right before God and no event, no opinion, no hostility, will harm you. The more solid your foundation—the deeper your root—the more steadfast you will be through the locust plagues of life.

1339. "If only I were free from these pressures, obligations, duties, debts, expectations, etc. blah blah. . . ."
    "Those may be hard to cast off. Yet at any moment you can free yourself from your own follies. If you really want liberation, why don't you act?"

1340. The goal of some people's lives is to have fun. That's not a conscious goal of mine because I have fun as a by-product of most of what I do. My life goal can be summed up as serving God by helping others, and I enjoy ("have fun") doing that.

1341. "Everything bears fruit." — Marcus Aurelius, 9.10
    The question is, Can your fruit be eaten?

1342. The better your learning, the better your eyes. — Proverb

1343. Tell me what you want and I'll tell you who you are. — Proverb

1344. Shall I compare thee to a piece of architecture? Art thou a wall, dark and high; or a cistern, empty and deep? Couldst thou be a tower from which to look, or perhaps best a bridge across the abyss of fear?

1345. Too many of us sit around worrying about our own feelings instead of getting off our butts and helping others. Work is the best therapy for a melancholy heart, anyway.

1346. Christians are called to be the *salt* of the earth, not the *sugar* of the earth.

1347. Some events have emotional meanings far beyond their strict logical value. There is, for example, a lot more than three minutes' difference between being at the gate when a loved one arrives on a plane and being three minutes' late. The logical value of handing someone a screwdriver from a table two feet away is small; its emotional value is large. Much happiness or unhappiness is determined by how well we understand these differences.

1348. A large goal of life should be to gain wisdom, for wisdom not only helps us to live better, happier, saner and more compassionate lives, but it also enables us to enhance the lives of others as we pass it on to them or at least gain some useful insights that help us serve them better. This said, it must be noted that wisdom is a product of reflection and focus—things that require time and peacefulness, thought without distraction. Our high-speed, high-pressure, dash-around society actually inhibits the formation of wisdom. We're too busy to be wise. Thus, in our anxiety to *do*, we neglect to *become*. Indeed, we're so busy doing everything that we neglect to become anything. I may have said this before but I'm too busy to check.

1349. Half the reason we're so cranky and discontent all the time is that we want an easy life rather than a constructive life. A constructive life—constructive to ourselves and to others—necessitates the measuring, sawing, and nailing that we rebel against. But do you want to build to the skies or lie flat?

1350. I would like to write this Glimmering as a tribute to books. Of course, for the ultimate praise, one should read Richard De

Bury's *Philobiblon*, but meanwhile I'd like to offer just a few words of my own. Books are good companions, for they do not desert you. When I've been rejected, I've turned to books for consolation and wisdom. When it is inconvenient for my friends to be around, a book is always available for some good conversation. When a book is near, I'm never bored and seldom lonely. When my mind is hungry, a feast is always ready for me, neatly packaged between two simple covers of cloth and cardboard. Who would think of eating cardboard and paper, and yet what greater feast is there than a good book?

1351. **Thoughts on reading *The Practice of the Presence of God* by Brother Lawrence:**

1. The path to spirituality need not begin with abstractions and discussions of faith, sin, justification, sanctification, mercy, grace, and so on. It can begin with concrete things, like flowers and butterflies and crystals.

2. We must not put God in a box marked "Spiritual Stuff." He is Lord of *all*. Whatever we are doing, God is there, willing to direct us if only we will ask.

3. Seek God for his own sake, not for the sake of what he can give you or do for you or forgive you for.

4. Whatever you do, do it because you love God, and everything you do will have value and worthiness.

5. Remember that God is our friend. And just as we feel comfortable and relaxed with a friend, speaking easily to him, so speak easily with God, discussing everything with him at any time during the day or night.

6. Virtue derives from the love of God. Virtue consists in behavior based on supra-individual principles—operating by rules beyond the self—either some abstract ideals or a focus on loving and honoring God. A good principle of behavior might be this: Do whatever you're willing to do while God, whom you love, is watching. Virtue depends on what you think—and do—when you are faced with temptation.

7. We should take time occasionally to think about who we are—to "enter into ourselves" and see what's there.

8. If, as Brother Lawrence says, love depends on knowledge and that "we must know before we can love," then there is no such thing as love at first sight—or rather, we mean something quite different by the use of the word "love" in that expression.

1352. We sometimes come to know things intuitively that we cannot articulate well logically. This may simply result from our lack of skill in communication and analysis. For example, a young lady, when asked why she loves a young man, may be reduced to giving an example she can remember: "When I made up a sandwich plate for a co-worker, he put some pretzels on it." What she really wants to say but cannot is that she loves him for his thoughtfulness and generosity of heart toward others, even those he doesn't know—he's a kind man, and this act is emblematic of that. His pretzels are indeed only one instance of a larger generality, but she can't quite get the abstraction right. So her audience, who hears only the single instance, takes it at face value and thinks she's a fool for loving someone "just for putting pretzels on a plate."

Many times, we love someone for "a thousand little things," each of which, by itself, would not be very impressive. That's why love is often difficult to explain.

1353. We will never find contentment and freedom from fear, worry, and anxiety until we realize that God is the only certainty, the only *permanent* friend.

1354. Life is a process where some people learn cynicism and others learn love.

1355. Ideas are more powerful than facts. —Proverb

1356. If God is already with you, why are you in such a hurry to get somewhere? If you already have God, why are you so worried and anxious about other things?

1357. Education is a process where you learn to ask better questions.

1358. Just as art is a metaphor for life, perhaps life itself is just a metaphor for reality.

1359. When experiencing something, the experience itself is gone even as it occurs. But every experience leaves something behind, in the mind. The question is, then, do you want to live for the sake of the experiences themselves or for the sake of what they leave behind? How you answer will determine how you live.

1360. Many married couples are too busy to be happy — too busily engaged in a struggle for power. For many, power is more seductive than sex. Too often, people who taste the wine of control cannot get enough. And they are willing to destroy the happiness of their relationship in order to get more.

1361. "I'm so upset with my husband. He never picks up his socks."
"I'm so upset with my wife. She always leaves the cap off the toothpaste."
"How long do you plan to stay married?"
"A long time."
"Yeah — for life."
"Then why are you being so petty?"

1362. Why people aren't happy:
1. They try to take shortcuts.
2. They want too much power.
3. They think about themselves too much.
4. They are proud.

We could add laziness, impatience, greed and so forth, but the above reasons pretty well sum up the root causes of "misery as a product of the ferocious search for happiness."

1363. The proverb, "Until you know what you're looking for, you can't find it," is both true and false. You might be looking for the book right in front of you, but if you don't know it, you won't find it. Ultimately what you're looking for, if only you knew it, might be the person or the bolt right at your elbow. On the other hand, often you don't and can't know what you're looking for until you see it. You might not know just what person or wallpaper you're looking for until you discover what's possible, or until an example—the right thing—resonates with something deep inside you that you never consciously suspected.

1364. Life is the search for connections. We live by seeking, making, and improving our associations. If we are too busy to feel connected, we are not living.

1365. Time, cash, and personal energy—these are your resources. What do you value enough to commit them to?

[June 11, 1992; age 41]

1366. Sometimes God is unsearchable. After all, he does say that his ways are higher than our ways. We just cannot always understand what he is doing or why he is doing it. Having faith "like a child" means that we should be curious, willing to learn, eager to understand; but when we are faced with things impossible to understand, we should accept the situation trustingly and not feel frustrated. That's what a child does.

1367. When you have a conflict with another person, a problem, or a challenge of any sort, you can take one of two approaches. Either you can work to defeat your opponent, or you can work to solve the problem. Understanding the difference between these two is important.

1368. What is the most real thing, the "ultimate reality"?

1369. To raise children well, to make your spouse happy, or to get along with your coworkers, just follow the golden triad:
    1. appreciate
    2. encourage
    3. forgive

1370. The golden key to making decisions is to know what your values are. Discussions in decision making theory about identifying and weighting criteria boil down to having clear values. The clearer your values, the easier making any decision will become. Thus a first step in becoming a manager or decision maker is to develop a clear and firm personal philosophy, a set of personal values that will guide you in whatever decision you must make.

Do you value generosity, efficiency, truth, profit, spiritual development, happiness, growth, power? How important is each value? And so forth.

What is the purpose of your life, your work, your job, your company? Do you have a corporate and a personal mission statement?

1371. If we are to be seekers of wisdom, we should answer some preliminary questions.
    1. What is wisdom?
    2. Why should we want to become wise?
    3. What effect does becoming wiser have on us?

Perhaps these questions must be answered by each person individually, but then perhaps they are universal after all. So here are some thoughts.

    1. Wisdom is the ability to see the best path through the forest and the desire to choose it. I hope this metaphor sums up the things involved with wisdom—insight, circumspection, discernment, good judgment, the ability to see things in context, humaneness, good values.

    2. We should want to become wise in order to be better servants of God, better servants of others, better parents, better workers, and better sojourners through life. We should desire to

be able to act and decide justly, fairly, beneficially.

3. Being wise should help us develop understanding, compassion, contentment, an improved soul, the ability to lead a more purposeful life. We will be able to help rather than harm others by our actions. We should be better able to face sorrow and joy, disaster and success.

If you think for a moment that every word you say and every deed you do will have some effect for more than a hundred thousand years (since your soul and the souls of others are affected thereby), you'd see the value of obtaining wisdom. Wisdom should be shared. Do you know something wise? Please tell me.

1372. If the fish would swim over to the boat and jump in, would fishing still be a sport? Would fishermen like it? No— there would be no challenge, no risk, no exhibition of skill, no possibility of failure, no possibility of improvement. We want challenge in our lives; we want to prove ourselves, to show how good we are.

1373. The purpose of life is not to grab the best slice of pizza before the person next to you can get it—that's just greed and selfishness. What we ought to do is choose the best slice and make sure someone else gets it. Why is this so hard for us to learn?

1374. **Ideas arising upon reading Dag Hammarskjold's *Markings*:**

1. Don't ask how good you are compared to other people; ask how good you are compared to what you can become.

2. "Friendship needs no words." But it often desires many words, for friends delight in sharing.

3. We are each such a little creature compared to the cosmos and to God—how can we think our deeds important? And yet our every act will have eternal consequences—how can we think our deeds are not important?

4. The only thing that can be really yours—yours forever—is that which you give to someone else.

5. The words of the living dead are life to the living dead. (The words of writers long dead give life to those alive in body but without values or purpose.)

6. You can't have friends unless you have values. Without values, all your interactions are merely responses to objects — alive or not. Thus, just as the key to decision making is personal values, so the key to friendship is also.

7. If you think that life is too unhappy, too limited, or too difficult, it is a sign that your heart, your imagination, and your problem solving ability are too restricted.

8. Most of us see others as means and ourselves as ends. We ought to see others as ends and ourselves as means.

9. "He was a member of the crew on Columbus's caravel — he kept wondering whether he would get back to his home village in time to succeed the old shoemaker before anybody else could grab the job." This is a portrait of human nature. We are often so obsessed with a predetermined idea for our future that we cannot realize the greatness of our present. We let pass the greatest of opportunities simply because we already have a lesser idea firmly in mind.

10. We don't always know when or how God is using us. A word of advice or encouragement, an offhand comment, a glance with a certain expression — God can use all of these in us to help or warn or teach others. Even as we sit idly and sip a cup of coffee, God may be using us as an example or model (good or bad!) to someone across the room. So we should pray that God will use us to enhance the lives of others, and we should strive to be the best models and helpers we can. But we shouldn't expect to know or recognize each occurrence.

11. In the process of making someone else good, you can't help but make yourself better.

12. "You can see how great I am by observing what I have done," said the chisel to the other tools, as they looked upon the beautiful statue.

13. All of your decisions are influenced by your belief about death.

1375. If we are humble, a word of criticism gives us a kindly word about how we can improve ourselves; if we are proud, a word of criticism gives us merely a reason to hate someone.

1376. Anxiety is a sign that you're counting on yourself rather than on God.

1377. If the salvation of your soul were the only purpose of your life, you could die when you were saved. But your soul is not perfect after salvation—it merely begins reconstruction. Life on earth prepares it for life after earth. But perhaps even more important, we're here to help others with the progress of their souls. Thus the old man's remark, "I can't die yet; there is still someone who needs my help."

1378. **Lessons from the Yucca Valley and Big Bear earthquakes:**
1. Being steadfast does not necessarily mean being rigid and inflexible. The ability to roll with the earthquake without moving from your foundation is the key to survival.
2. The news media have no concept of degree in disasters. All events are essentially alike—"terrible tragedies," "devastating earthquakes," "massive destruction." What terms will they use when something *really* bad happens?

1379. There is meaning in everything if we attune ourselves to it. Why then do we seek and discard one thing after another in an endless search for "meaning"?

1380. It's not what you know but what you apply.

1381. When you die, you hope to have left your mark on the world—but will it be a directional arrow or a scar?

1382. The spider who spins his web in a dead location—an abandoned house, a tightly closed cupboard—starves to death. He hopes but starves. Thus is ambition without analysis.

1383. It is important not only to have a goal but not to lose sight of it.

1384. The young woman sat on her knees silently just a few feet from the man she loved, waiting in case he needed something. She had been sitting this way for four hours. And yet she did not think, "Am I above this?" "Am I bored?" "Should I leave?" "Can I do better?" Instead, she thought, "How I love him."

1385. "The central work of life is interpretation." —Joseph M. Ricke

Every event, every situation, needs to be interpreted both for its fundamental nature (exactly what it is or what happened) and for our attitude toward it. Often these two interpretations intermingle, making it critical for us to place a just meaning on what happens. Thus, the really important thing in life is not merely having an experience or learning about it, but interpreting it well.

Suppose you must drive to a distant airport to take a plane for your destination. You can think, "Oh, no, I have to drive to Distantville; what a pain." Or you can think, "Oh boy, here's a neat opportunity for something different, exciting, fun, adventurous." This is more than just seeing problems as opportunities; it is the difference between whiny, unhappy people and cheerful optimists.

Interpretation is further important because you must ask, "What does this mean?" or "How important is this?" before you can make a decision to act.

1386. Selection is a creative act.

1387. One of these days I'll write a proverb about procrastination.

1388. The moment you cease to serve others, your heart begins to rust.

1389. Hoarding is squandering.

1390. What's the difference between the dead and the idle? The dead are no longer wasting the earth's resources.

1391. Don't think about how much you can get with what you have, but how much you can give from what you have.

1392. "A better mixdown isn't going to turn this slop into music," said the recording engineer.

"Then it's time to push all the sliders forward," said the promoter.

1393. Perhaps a better question than, "How will you experience your future?" is, "How will you experience your past?" For your past and your interpretation of it control your perceptions and beliefs and assumptions. Your past has taught you—not necessarily correctly—what can be done, who is good, what is to be feared, what is possible, what can be known, what should be pursued, and so forth.

1394. **What are the ten most important sayings of all time?** Here are some candidates:

1. Put God first.
2. Know Thyself.
3. It is not right to do evil in order to bring about good.
4. This too shall pass.
5. The more you get, the more you have; the more you give, the more you are.
6. Not the event, but the attitude.
7. Look to the end.
8. Seize opportunity.
9. Moderation in all things. The middle road is best.
10. Love your neighbor as yourself. (In other words, be a servant.)

The classical virtues are prudence, temperance, justice, fortitude. The Christian virtues are faith, hope, charity.

[November 2, 1992; age 42]

1395. Life is a search for better instrumentation.
[Because instruments are interpreters and guides — they tell us about our environment and help us to negotiate its labyrinths. They warn us of excesses and deficiencies.]

1396. "If your mind is not looking, your eyes will see nothing."
— Publilius Syrus

1397. Few things are as constant as our need for reassurance.

1398. Some people will laugh at an insane man because he is completely disengaged from reality. And yet many of these same people are rescued from their own laughter only by the word "completely."

1399. In Chaos Theory, the Butterfly Effect posits that the world weather system is so sensitive that a butterfly flapping its wings in an isolated meadow can cause the difference between rain and sunshine ten thousand miles away a week later. I think this same effect can be applied to the influence people have on the world spiritually and culturally. A small act of kindness or cruelty may substantially change the course of civilization through an ever-linking chain reaction and an ever-enlarging snowball effect. Thus, there are no insignificant actions and no insignificant people.

1400. The problem with the modern secular world is that ontological preferences are presented as epistemological necessities — and with such a self righteousness as to make one ill. The problem with the modern Christian world is the failure to conform personal practice with personal belief. Instead of allowing their faith to regulate their actions, too many Christians allow secular social norms to dictate their behavior.

1401. Is God invisible? The answer depends on what you mean by the question. His being or person is invisible to us as being or person, but other parts of the creation, such as angels, can see him. But more importantly for us, God is visible everywhere through his creation and his activities—in butterfly wings, in the song of birds, in the structure of salt crystals. He is visible through a loving caress, a mother's smile, or through the guy that stops his car and gets out his jumper cables to help a stranded motorist.

1402. The engineers sitting in the booth in a recording studio don't hear what is actually being played by the band; they hear an adjusted version, set to their tastes. Everyone's brain is a little recording booth where the sliders are arranged in a unique pattern, depending on the interests of the person. When we pay attention to or are concerned with a special aspect of reality, we push that slider a little farther forward, amplifying the prominence of that aspect. The same is true when we are not interested in something: we pull the slider back a bit or mute that aspect altogether. Thus, none live in reality as it is performed—we live in our preferred version of it. In fact, insofar as possible, we select the band and the music they play—our public experiences.

If you want to test this easily, buy a red car. Soon you'll see how many red cars are on the road. Or buy a restaurant. You'll suddenly see restaurant signs everywhere.

1403. It is always the right time to begin to be wise.

1404. He who understands a crack in the wall will not be found dead in the rubble. —after Publilius Syrus

1405. The beginning of wisdom is the recognition that you need it. —after Publilius Syrus

1406. For no one can sing a song that doesn't exist or quote a poem that hasn't been written. Go forth and create your art as a gift to the future.

1407. Sometimes each of us is afraid to know the truth; at those times, when we insist upon knowing the truth anyway, we reveal our spiritual nature.

1408. When God is with you, you can cross the ocean on a twig. —after Publilius Syrus

1409. What the uneducated see as the new truth that sweeps out the old error or the outdated truth, the thoughtful see as merely a parallel model that describes the universe in an alternative way.

1410. Some people want a place to stand so they can change the world, but most people just want a comfortable place to sin.

1411. We are actors all—seeking opportunities that will allow us to reach out of the confinements of our personalities and try new roles. Thus we sing in the choir, act in a play, teach a class, play with children—whatever we can that will make it socially or psychologically acceptable to move beyond our ordinary selves.

1412. Not just the thing but the quality of the thing determines its value. Jewelry, art, literature, automobiles—all these must be rated for quality. Thus the ability to recognize quality is a highly valuable skill, the only means to keep from being swindled. This truth applies to people as well.

1413. If the wine is good, no need to brag about the awards it has won. It will sell because of its taste, not its reputation.

1414. How you say something is even more important than what you say, for while what you say acts upon the mind, how you say it acts upon the ego. It is a greater feat to get past the ego than it is to get past the intellect.

1415. Back in the old days—50 or 100 years ago—little things mattered. Bricks, for example, were carefully molded and even stamped with the maker's name: SOMERS. Now, even the idea of brand-name bricks or pride in quality brickmaking seems almost absurd. So we get bricks not as well made, though still functional enough. Thus does civilization decline. "It still works," or "That's good enough," we say. By losing our desire or ability to care about little things—punctuation, thank-you notes, a well-made sandwich—our lives become gradually, accumulatively, inexorably less.

[July, 1993; age 42]

1416. Thus does an old man pause longer and more meditatively than a young man at a scenic vista, not merely because the old man possesses a greater store of associations or is wiser or is in less of a hurry or because he can discern more or because he has already seen what the young man is eager yet to discover in another location—no, the old man pauses because he knows that for those propelled by the hunger of imagination, the journey *is* the destination.

[November 30, 1993; age 43]

1417. If you learn from your own mistakes, you gain experience; if you learn from someone else's mistakes, you gain wisdom.

1418. "In the midst of myriad truth, yet a hunger for meaning." We have facts, but we need truth. We have truth, but we need meaning. They ask for meaning and we give them data. "With all your knowledge, get understanding." The hierarchy is data, information, facts, knowledge, truth, understanding, wisdom, values. The empirical ceiling occurs approximately at the interface between facts and knowledge. Everything after that is qualitative, perhaps subjective, at least non-empirical, not provable.

1419. Man is a fool, but only a wise man knows this.

1420. The illness of modern man is that for him, God is little more than a mildly amusing intellectual construct.

1421. So we learn from chaos theory that science is driven by philosophy. Is that something we didn't know before?

[January 22, 1994; age 43]

1422. Patience is the persistence of the powerless.

1423. He truly has understanding who knows when to hold on and when to let go.

1424. "Wise is the man who has two loaves and sells one to buy a lily." —Chinese proverb

1425. The goal of education is not to teach you how to get what you want; the goal of education is to teach you what to want. (With thanks to Menedemus.)

1426. How many people want to get rich quickly, or to rise to power rapidly, or to possess immediate pleasure. But how many ever express the desire for the speedy acquisition of wisdom? "I am engaged in an urgent quest for wisdom."

1427. Wisdom is often defined as judgment or discernment. But it is also contained in the ability to make penetrating comments on life, to have compassion, circumspection, understanding. Knowledge will help you function; wisdom will help you live.

1428. When we return to a place we loved in our youth, our shock and sadness are produced not so much by how different the place is physically—the trees gone, the stream replaced by houses—as by the realization that we were attempting to return to a memory, and that, even if the place had remained physically the same, we could still not recapture that same feeling of aliveness we once had.

1429. Ideas, at their birth, are often the most fragile things in the universe. We must therefore be careful whom we share them with, lest they be ravaged or killed by ridicule, laughter, scorn, or simple opposition. The encourager of a new idea, on the other hand, is a hero, a partaker in the process of creation, who can give strength not only to that idea but to the idea-having process.

It is true that ideas ultimately need to be evaluated and the bad ones dropped or changed, but when the idea process is just beginning, the first blush of a thought is frequently bad or silly or imperfect from a ruthlessly objective viewpoint. But good ideas often come from bad ideas. That is the stepping stone principle.

1430. A lone critic is a crank; two critics are a movement; three critics are a revolution.

1431. Two men lived long and worked hard, one in the foreground of life and one in the background. At the first man's death, a hundred and twenty-seven cars followed his hearse to the cemetery, and as his soul entered heaven two angels applauded deliberately. At the second man's death, four cars followed his hearse to the cemetery, and as his soul entered heaven a thousand angels sang praises while someone said, "Well done, good and faithful servant."

1432. **Lessons from a Marriage, Part 1.**
1. Respect your spouse's privacy. Even though you may frequently chase each other through the house naked, be considerate of the other person's need for personal space and private moments. If the bathroom door is closed, don't just walk in; knock first. The issue is not secrecy, but respect.

2. Don't tease too much. Most teasing these days involves negative comments and criticisms; even positive teasing comes off as sarcastic and is therefore taken negatively. While a little teasing can be fun, a little goes a long way, and the criticism can build up. The saying, "There is a little truth in every tease," may or may not be absolutely correct; but sensitive people, especially, see truth in every critical comment. Your spouse may laugh at your teasing, but be hurting inside.

3. It is not necessary to comment on every lapse by your spouse. Some partners think they are "helping" their spouses remember when they say things like, "You didn't turn off the light," "You forgot to put the mug on the shelf," or "You didn't fold your towel." The torrent of criticism resulting from this helpfulness will not do your relationship any good. It is better just to turn off the light, put the mug on the shelf, and just let the towel hang as is. If your spouse leaves the lights on habitually, sit down and discuss the matter. Is that intentional, forgetful, the lack of a habit, or what? Single criticisms, sometimes from the next room, are often taken as potshots at the person, because they are clearly seen as unnecessary.

4. Don't make any statement that begins, "You never. . . ." It's obviously intended as an insult, and insults are not helpful.

5. Try to use "we" instead of "I" or "you" whether you are bragging or complaining.

1433. One of the paradoxes of life is that young people, who have all their years ahead of them, are always impatient for every action; while old people, who have little time on earth left, seem often unhurried and willing to wait.

1434. Wisdom must be more than a knowledge of the proper objects of pursuit and contemplation. A wise man who never moves and never speaks is one who never gives: he is only half wise. Wisdom must be an activity. Part of wisdom is understanding: to understand the conflicts in our own hearts and to understand the choices others make. And part of wisdom is active: the ability to make good decisions and to set worthy goals.

1435. "What's that idiot doing now?" said the woman, whose ignorance alone made her resentful as a harmless man walked by. People like her are their own punishment, for they have to live with themselves. [On the road to Hana during a traffic delay, May 1992, I being the referenced "idiot."]

1436. What you would destroy, first make boring. Presenting something as boring is perhaps even more effective than laughing at it as a means of eliminating it from serious consideration.

1437. "The most important thing is what *really* happened."

"No, that's of tertiary importance."

"Of course. It's what *you think* happened that's most important, right?"

"No, that's secondary."

"Okay, so what's primary?"

"The most important part of an event is your response to it."

"Huh?"

"What actually happens shapes the outside world, which is even now changing and passing away. What you think has happened shapes the world of knowledge—or of belief about knowledge—which will soon be supplanted by newer and more accurate ideas. How you respond to what you think happened shapes your soul and thus has a permanent, an eternal, effect."

"So what happens to you doesn't matter."

"Of course it matters. But how you make it matter is the issue."

1438. Life is an ongoing struggle to adjust the idealism of youth to the reality of a clearly imperfect world. The adjustment can take the form of resentment, anger, bitterness, cynicism, resignation, surrender, resistance, expediency—or, one can see that the world is an endless source of opportunity.

1439. You can't really change someone else. The most you can do is give someone insight into his actions, behavior, or personality—and hope he will use that knowledge to attempt self adjustment.

1440. Artistic judgments are often political rather than esthetic judgments. A painting, book, or film is praised or ignored because it reflects a philosophy the critic likes or dislikes rather than because the work possesses or lacks real artistic merit. This fact of life derives partly from the modern unwillingness to judge anything on the basis of a standard—of taste, merit, esthetics—and partly because the world is highly political.

"Why do you think Smervitz won the academy award for best director? Because of his subtle handling of the love scene? The multiple camera angles of the journey across the plains? The slow motion effects of the explosion?"

"No, it was just time for him to win. He has made a lot of politically correct films and hadn't won yet. So the academy gave him the award."

1441. People sometimes respond differently to the same situation, often with shock and disbelief, because they have different mental models by which they understand the situation. For example, suppose Bill and Jane are sitting in a hot tub together. Bill's mental model of a hot tub is that of a flowing hot spring, up in the mountains, where he can sit out in the cool air and relax in the pristine water. Jane's mental model is that a hot tub is rather like a communal bathtub, filled with dirty bathwater from a hundred previous occupants—in fact, she is sitting in Bill's bathwater and feels rather unclean. Thus, when Bill dips his head under water, he is dipping into a flowing stream in his mind, while Jane sees him dipping his head into a toilet. She is horrified and he can't understand why.

Such differences in the way we conceptualize various situations cause a lot of difficulty. The problem is not misunderstanding; it is different understanding, or a lack of understanding the other person's model.

1442. To say, "I did not find it," is not the same as to say, "It was not there." Only in our pride do we equate these.

1443. The clutter of our daily activity is dust on the mirror of life.

1444. Sign over a bathtub: "Cleanse your heart each day as well."

1445. Memory is sequential. Thus a road seems unfamiliar when driven the opposite way or when begun on a part that isn't usually driven.

1446. "Timing is the key." We realize this when we listen to a musician or even a whole orchestra playing all the right notes, period. We are beings of rhythm, of synchronization, of ripeness. A mistimed word can be worse than silence.

1447. **The Observer's Vignette No. 1.**
They went out, in the cool night, to the courtyard of the mall and sat on the side and listened to the loud band and smoked cigarettes and didn't talk much. The people they saw who were like them didn't talk much.

One or two would have liked some coffee, but no one said it would have been good, so no one had any. Others like them were eating ice cream, so they ordered ice cream. A couple of the girls were cold and thought that ice cream on a cold night was dumb, but they didn't say anything except to name a flavor which was one of the flavors their friends had ordered.

1448. Living by imitation: "If others are enjoying this, we must be enjoying it, too." The *idea* of enjoyment is more significant in many decisions than experienced enjoyment. I hate to say it, but I think Samuel Johnson might have been wrong when he said, "No man is a hypocrite in his pleasures." Such hypocrisy is rampant in adolescence, and how many there are who never quite outgrow that period.

1449. "Does this contribute to your long term goals?" Well, possibly. For someone who is curious, who loves technology, who learns by analogy, who tells stories in class to teach or to make a point, who can use any realistic detail to embellish a story—for someone like this, even apparently peripheral experiences can contribute toward long term goals. All knowledge can be useful, and variety of knowledge and experience are valuable for the circumspection and general awareness we all need.

1450. Lots of people speak frequently about "the spiritual" dimension in things. "Find your inner spirit," they say. Is this a substitute for God or a pathway to him?

1451. Lessons from a Marriage, Part 2.

6. When your spouse shares ideas with you, don't object to, disagree with, criticize, or otherwise judge every idea. Ideas are fragile things and they also are seen as parts of ourselves, until we change or reject them ourselves. If your responses are constantly negative, your spouse will find someone else to talk to.

7. Give your spouse opportunity to talk. Don't talk for half an hour and then say, "Now you talk." People cannot talk on demand, especially when they have been trying to attend to a raging river of words from someone else. Show by frequent pauses and inquiring facial expressions that you are open to a response to your statements. And be sure to allow your spouse to start conversations once in awhile, to name and pursue a subject. In other words, don't always talk about yourself or your own experience. The old, "So how was your day?" actually has some use.

8. Don't try to remake your spouse into another copy of yourself. The saying is, "You can't change others, so change yourself." Only others can change themselves, and it's not your duty to "help" others change. You are a husband or a wife, not a mother to your spouse.

9. When you are away from each other and talk on the telephone, be as positive and loving as you can and try to avoid anything critical or negative. Your spouse will not have your pres-

ence to undo any negative feelings you create during a conversation on the phone, and will have a picture of you in your "telephone mood" until the next contact. If you are critical, and the next contact is two days later, that's two days of criticism you have subjected your spouse to.

1452. If education is, in fact, a process of disillusionment, where do the illusions come from?

1453. There is a connection between maturity and humility. For example, the immature criticize what they do not understand, thinking they need no more knowledge or insight to make a judgment. The mature still may not understand, but they realize there may be circumstances they do not know, or they know that their preferences are not the standard of the world. The immature believe that whatever is not their way is the wrong way (a prideful position indeed), while the mature realize that tastes and standards differ. Compassion, sympathy, empathy — these come from a mature mind and a humble heart.

1454. "If a tree falls where no one can hear, did it make a noise?"
— Ancient Philosophical question.
    If an event happens where there is no journalist or communication link, did it happen? Is it news? Is it significant? "Important news" is selected from the pool of events that are available, that are known.

1455. Those who speak much please themselves; those who listen much please others. Those who speak much receive smiles; those who listen much receive wisdom.

1456. In the external world — the world of professional relationships and business, what you do is more important than what you say. Hence the criticism, "All talk and no action." But in the internal world, the world of close personal relationships, what you say is often more important than what you do. Hence the saying, "A stick hurts for an hour, but a word can hurt for years." Just a few small critical comments can cause more hurt than many gifts or even kisses can erase.

1457. A dream of what will be or what might be allows us to plan to seek or to avoid a particular future.

1458. Marriage vows to love, honor, cherish, and be generally kind to each other are so often not kept simply because vows come from the head or the heart—with good intentions, certainly—while the spouses' everyday behavior toward each other comes from their personalities. If people wouldn't promise to behave differently from what their personality will permit, there would be fewer disappointments in relationships. And fewer relationships, of course.

1459. Don't ask, "How well does this measure up to the standard of quality?" Ask rather, "Will this help advance the standard of quality?"

1460. Many people fall in love, and a lucky few even become friends.

1461. A common error is to think that things give value to people. Hence, fancy suits, expensive cars, and jewelry are seen as marks of the important. But the reality is that people give value to things. Unless people agree to value a thing, the thing has no value.

1462. Sometimes truth starts with knowledge, but often it comes through experience. Action leads to belief, to knowledge, to understanding. Truth must be discovered or worked out through experiment. Truth is what you do with who you are.

1463. Pride is the principal obstacle to truth. Pride is a major barrier to happiness. Pride is a large source of cruelty. Pride inhibits the capacity to love. The fruit of humility is gentleness, compassion, kindness, generosity, a desire to learn, to love, to trust—even to take risks.

1464. If you start to feel self-satisfied, your soul is moving in the wrong direction.

1465. They want to live long, they want to live with wealth and power, but they do not want to know how to live.

1466. "Tell me what you want and I'll tell you who you are" is a good piece of wisdom. But there is more: "Tell me why you seek what you do and I'll tell you what you will become." What you seek is important, but why you seek it is even more important.

[July 4, 1994; age 43]

1467. "It is our duty to live among books." —John Henry Newman
   For we are obligated by our humanity and as thinking beings to share intelligent conversation for our own betterment, and where can the average armchair philosopher find intelligent conversation but in books?

1468. Reading and thinking are not idleness. They are better activities than many of the physical busynesses most people indulge in.

1469. Many of the ancient philosophers (Aristotle, Epicurus, Lucretius etc., etc.) wrote books of theoretical physics, thus showing the importance of cosmogony and ontology for the foundation of ethics. The way we believe the physical universe is constituted affects the way we believe the moral universe is constituted.

1470. **The Observer's Vignette No. 2.**
   Her view of reality is constructed from the pages of the su-

permarket tabloids, but she considers herself rational because she lives in modern times. She knows the person she has heard about is guilty or innocent because she just feels it. How good it is to think clearly, she says to herself as she leaves the store with a bag of tortilla chips and a six pack of diet soda.

1471. Lessons from a Marriage, Part 3.

10. When you apologize for hurting your spouse's feelings or for doing something wrong, do not attempt to justify your words or actions as part of the apology. Do not say, for example, "I'm sorry for yelling at you, but you were acting stupid." Such statements are not apologies, but continued criticisms, aggressive self justifications, continued displays of ego — while an apology implies some sense of humility as well as regret. It is better not to apologize at all than to talk thusly.

11. Don't use a scornful or irritated tone of voice when your spouse asks a question you think he or she should know the answer to or when he or she asks the same question again. Many people are forgetful; they don't ask questions without wanting an answer.

12. Keep your spouse's confidences. Do not tell even your best friend the personal details your spouse confides in you. If you betray this trust even once, don't expect your spouse to open up to you again. Men especially will avoid sharing their vulnerabilities with a wife who shares them with others.

1472. There is a tendency in human nature, related to pride but stemming from insecurity, to ridicule whatever we have just left behind — whether puberty, a spouse, a job, high school, even religion. Condemning the past seems to be part of breaking away.

1473. Few decisions are made with certainty, even when made with decisiveness. There is always a bit of doubt in our minds. But that is what choice is all about.

1474. Every choice is a test, a ruler that measures you.

1475. "The wise man will leave written words behind him," says Epicurus.

1476. "All knowledge is accompanied by pain," says Aristotle. Here are some more facts about knowledge:

1. People do not want to know everything. They fear some knowledge.

2. People cannot know something that they believe cannot be known. Their prejudices prevent them from learning many things.

3. People want new knowledge to support what they already believe. Their bias directs their search.

4. People want to be comfortable in their knowledge. They do not want disturbing knowledge.

1477. **Lessons from a Marriage, Part 4.**

13. Don't use your spouse's every lapse as an opportunity to sneer or criticize: "I can't find my comb." "Well, if you kept it where it belongs, it wouldn't get lost." Or "Are we leaving at five or six?" "Why would we leave at five — three hours early?"

14. Don't blame your spouse for every problem. "Look how the weeds stuck to this blanket. If we'd brought the towels like I suggested, this wouldn't have happened." "Look at this traffic jam. Why did you take this street anyway? The other road is never this crowded."

1478. "The wise man is grateful when he is corrected," says Epicurus.

This is one of the most challenging statements of philosophy.

1479. You can't say you know much about a person until you've seen him in at least three roles, because most people are role players. What seems to be a kind or stern or brainless person may, in another setting, be quite different. The roles a person plays as a father, mother, husband, wife, son, daughter, brother, sister, or leader or follower may be quite different.

Different constraints and different amounts of relative power influence our behavior.

1480. Lessons from a Marriage, Part 5.

15. Don't criticize your spouse in public. Public criticism (whether in the general public or in front of friends) implies that you are trying to enlist others against your spouse. It is also humiliating to your spouse to be publicly shamed.

16. Don't grudge your spouse's pleasures. If she likes romance novels, don't complain, "I don't know why you bring that junk into the house." If he collects match books, don't complain, "I don't know why you want to keep all that worthless stuff." Many people seek to augment what little joy they are having in life by adding a few harmless pleasures that others may not understand. Don't make their small pleasure yet one more source of misery.

17. Choose your words. Thoughtless words can do just as much damage as any intentionally cruel ones.

1481. We often talk about the power of sex and the power of love (and even confuse the two), but we seldom discuss the power of hatred or the power of the desire for excitement and amusement. Network and local TV news, horror movies, amusement parks, vacation spots — all are influenced by and feed our desire for excitement and amusement.

1482. With a natural attraction, such as beautiful scenery, the location is the attraction. With an artificial attraction, like Las Vegas or Disneyland, the event is the attraction. Most attractions are partly esthetic and partly kinesthetic. Natural attractions usually emphasize the esthetic (though you can hike, boat, etc.), while artificial attractions usually emphasize the kinesthetic (though you can admire the architecture, lights, decor). Exceptions would be museums (mostly esthetic) and water areas (often kinesthetic because people like to swim, sail, water ski, etc.).

In all this, people determine what is attractive to themselves, and personalities differ. Extroverts usually like kinesthetic amusements; introverts usually like esthetic ones.

1483. Meaning is often constructed rather than discovered. A group of people determine by an act of will what is important or memorable. They gather in a spot and put up a rock and declare that it has meaning. Memory sustains meaning. When we forget, meaning is lost.

1484. We regard as heroes the firsts—the initiators, the explorers—because doing something new and different is hard: it means change and deviation from the norm and often initial social disapproval. Many heroes had to hear, "What do you think you're doing?" before they heard, "Hey, that's great!"

1485. "That was a cold service. I got nothing out of it." Which raises the question, Who is responsible for your religious experience? The pastor? The congregation? Or perhaps—you?

And secondly, what is a religious experience? Is it a feeling? Or a thought? Most people seem to equate religious experience with emotion, but why? Cannot it be an intellectual experience? Or a person-to-person experience with a Friend? I don't feel all emotional when I have lunch with my friend P—. Cannot I commune with my Friend Jesus without feeling all mushy, too? (I don't object to feeling—I sometimes have remarkable emotion when praying. But I don't usually. I simply want to point out that religious experience can be more than or other than emotional in nature and quality.)

1486. **Thoughts After Reading Suetonius.**
1. Civilization exists in individuals rather than in societies or political structures. Nero and Seneca lived at the same time. Culture and civilization are created and preserved by a person here and a person there, not by governmental decree. In fact, a plurality of cultures exists, some good, some bad, many simply hedonistic.

2. The unlimited indulgence of the ego leads to insanity. Thus, humility is sanity.

3. The principal marks of civilization must be (a) honesty and integrity (for trust is the glue that holds society together), (b) justice, fairness, due process, protection by law, and (c) mutual respect for persons, their safety, and their property. We hope that a rich culture can be added to this, as well as a reliable food supply, exchange of ideas, and so on.

4. Examples of shrewd judgments: When a woman refused to admit that she was the mother of a man in court, Claudius ordered her to marry the man, forcing her to confess. When a man was accused of posing as a Roman citizen, Claudius ordered him to wear a Greek mantle when accused and a Roman gown when defending himself. When a dispute arose over who owned a transport animal, Galba ordered it to be led blindfolded to its trough and then, unblindfolded, allowed to go to one person or the other of its own accord.

1487. "Dishonest success is the same as failure," says Hesiod, in *Works and Days.*

1488. A brace of couplets:

> Not wisdom known, but practiced, is the rule
> That separates the wise man from the fool.

> Give thanks, ye proud, to Him whose mighty hand
> Created mankind from a fist of sand.

1489. "You can't see the whole sky through a bamboo tube."
—Japanese proverb

1490. "The hardest person to awaken is the person already awake." —Filipino proverb

1491. Many of the new software programs have an undo button that allows the user to reverse the last selection or operation. A few programs permit undoing the last 100 operations. That's just what we need for our personal lives: an unchoose button. Many times we want to unsay, unvolunteer, unselect, or undo an action. Would that we could.

1492. Progress is made by one person who perseveres with an idea. Others stand around and clap with one hand or stare with incredulity or even offer perfunctory praise for the effort. But one person champions the idea, pushes for it, works at it. Only after the idea is successful do people stop asking, "What's his problem?" and start offering material help.

1493. Joy makes us want to go out and share with others; grief makes us want to be alone. People who have grief feel that they have been singled out for pain, that they are alone and must suffer by themselves. The comfort for grief, then, is simply to spend time with the griever. If you have experienced a similar pain, you might share that: "My son, too, is ill"; "I had that problem in my own life." Don't say, "Lots of people have that problem." Just let the sufferer know, "You're not alone. I'm here with you."

1494. "How you live is the key."
   "Who you are will determine how you live."
   "Whom you serve will shape who you are and thus how you live."

1495. What causes highly educated intellectuals and scholars to fail or to go wrong in their search for truth? Their thinking and analysis are based on assumptions, unexamined or unrecognized, and the assumptions are wrong. Secondly, their conclusions suffer from faulty interpretation. The discernment of correct meaning is more than a product of knowledge or education. Personal values and worldview are critical.

1496. Are you writing your own life or is your life mostly quotation? And if it is borrowed from others, is that less or more than an utterly original life? The rebel who lives like no one ever lived does not necessarily have a better life.

1497. Few people are listening; everyone is watching.

1498. My mother the philosopher: After her mentally ill son has lived with her for a dozen years in her old age, though he yells curses to the skies and pounds on the furniture, he is, she says, some company, and taking care of him gives her life activity. Her conclusion: "Sometimes a burden is also a blessing." The reverse is no doubt true, too, as those who have won the lottery can probably attest: "Sometimes a blessing is also a burden." Thus is life a strange phenomenon.

1499. The first rule of interpersonal relationships is, Give them room to move. People must not be transfixed by pins and stuck in our albums of permanently defined things. A person's personality is not fixed; it is a process. If, when you meet someone, you realize that you are meeting a personality process rather than a static character, you'll be more likely to allow that person to change.

1500. **The Observer's Vignette, No. 3.**
    They sit in a group and make an effort to produce a convincing laugh, though all that comes is a bitter chuckle. The gaiety of their lives has passed away with the loss of innocence; their somber outlook reflects the burden of guilt, though they don't feel guilty in any way: they have followed the mores of popular culture; so for what deed should they feel any guilt? Yet in their eyes there is a sadness only partly disguised.

1501. The first sign of wisdom occurs when you stop measuring other people by yourself.

1502. Oh, the patience of books. They wait quietly for the ripening season of our minds. A book will sit by without complaint for years, until suddenly a stimulus hits us and we want to read it: finally, we ask the question the book can answer, or we are interested in the question.

1503. Wisdom must begin with a question, a doubt, a humility. An age that worships pride, the self, cannot be wise. Thus, "The fear of the Lord is the beginning of wisdom."

1504. Why wisdom? Solomon prayed for wisdom so he could act well, choose well, live well.

1505. **Lessons from a Marriage, Part 6.**
18. Allow your spouse as much autonomy as possible. Don't try to control, determine, or even influence everything your spouse does or thinks. Don't insist that he or she clean out or arrange every drawer and shelf to suit you. It is especially important to leave your spouse personal space: a desk, sewing room, closet, workshop, etc.

1506. The Greeks were right when they spoke of *ethos*. It all comes down to relationships. Others must have respect for your life before they will respect your message or beliefs. Politicians could learn from this. So could teachers and preachers.

1507. Why don't evangelicals shape culture? (1) They believe they are "too good" for the "secular" arts and media. They don't want to be tainted; they believe the arts aren't very valuable; they are anti-intellectual and anti-cultural. (2) They believe that all emphasis should be on direct evangelization. They do not realize the value of pre-evangelism or of a value-rich cultural background on which to build the faith.

1508. The flower is not content merely to beautify the world it knows; it leaves seeds to beautify many worlds it will never know.

[January 27, 1995; age 44]

1509. Why is it that the least creative people find new ideas so obvious, while the truly creative respond with praise and enthusiasm?

1510. "A wise man can know ten things by learning one."
—Japanese Proverb

1511. There are three categories of things to do: have to, ought to, want to. After the have to, we often use the rest of our time on the ought to, instead of the want to. I say, put your time where your heart is. We can never satisfy all the oughts of our lives anyway.

1512. We are all investors: only our choice of investment and our expected dividends differ. Some invest in stocks, some in people; some invest in the future, some in the past. Perhaps that is the meaning of "Where your treasure is, there will your heart be also."

1513. If you are only against something, you will ultimately fail. The practice of searching out a proposed or actual wrong and rallying a crowd to oppose it may work for the occasion, but ultimately your ideals will be pushed to the periphery of existence. Civilization moves forward by following ideas, not by following opposition to ideas. Progress requires a positive vision, an impetus in a productive direction. Always remember, then, that when you are against something, the most important argument is what you are for.

1514. Those who sit in the seat of judgment are not always wise or perceptive or chosen from among men because of their discernment and probity. And sometimes the judges' decisions are designed to validate previous judgments or to exalt their own position, rather than to be a true evaluation of the case before them.

1515. That beautiful, old, hand-finished dresser, an heirloom, a priceless antique, a family treasure — becomes a pile of firewood either by a sorry accident (dropping it off the truck on the freeway) or simply by a change of attitude, a redefinition. "That's nice, but it wasn't my grandma's," or "Well, this is a fake of recent origin" — such a comment creates a radical revision. Conversely, even a matchbook cover that grandpa collected or a small stone found on a walk with a loved one can be invested with great and lasting value. Thus, value is an attitude or a belief, not a fact existing objectively in an object.

A major activity of the intellectual world is the constant process of ascribing value to some things (ideas, concepts, theories, art objects, actions, historical events) and denying value to others. The reputations of ideas are constantly under enhancement or diminishment in a process more political than scientific. Opinion rules the world, someone has said.

1516. If you criticize someone or something too much, others will lose respect for *you*, rather than for what you criticize.

1517. "I will make a pilgrimage in search of wisdom," said a man to his friend. "It must be somewhere."

"How will you find wisdom elsewhere, when you cannot find it here?" asked his friend. "You do not find wisdom with your feet; you find it with your eyes. Wisdom comes from how you see the everyday world around you."

"I see," said the man.

"No you don't," replied his friend.

1518. In that country the intellectuals no longer questioned anything: all they did was reject and scorn. They were determined to find the world meaningless, and to find good as nothing but an empty shell or a vapor. And they were deeply resentful that the people could find little use for intellectuals.

1519. The statement, "I don't care," is the first sign of old age.

1520. The young man plops the blank into the lathe, twirls a dial, and punches the On button. Soon a nice-looking bat or chair leg emerges, and the young man looks at it with satisfaction. The old man is slower: he puts the blank in carefully, aligning it once, twice, and then gently clamping it down. He, too, soon finds a nicely made bat or chair leg, but when he removes it from the lathe, he feels the wood, the texture; he even enjoys the smell of the cut. The look on his face is one of admiration, too — not for the cut, but for the wood itself. And so what? The young man has added to the inventory; the old man has added to life.

1521. The dream of many a professor is someone who is really interested, someone who wants to learn, who values knowledge, who feels the same gratification of learning that he feels. Someone who resonates with the proverbs of learning:
- The better your learning, the better your eyes.
- The more you know, the more you can feel.
- No learning, no quality.
- Knowledge paves the road to the door of understanding; the door of understanding opens to the palace of wisdom.
- Knowledge is the friend of happiness.

1522. The good thinker can identify the difficulties involved with a proposal; the better thinker can discover ways of overcoming them.

1523. Instead of thinking of yourself, you should think about yourself. Examine your heart to see what you value, what motivates you, what you desire, what future you see for yourself. Understand yourself in order to improve and lead yourself.

1524. **Lessons from reading Francis Bacon's *Essays*:**
    1. For some people, commitment is slavery. Thus the refusal to commit to another in a relationship, and the refusal to commit to a position or belief. [Of Truth]
    2. We are made happier by a small profit than by waiting for a large one. So if you can do nothing else today, create or copy a

small piece of wisdom. [Of Empire]

3. To be happy, wise, popular, well thought of, pleasing to others: talk less and ask more questions. [Of Discourse]

4. "The causes of superstition are: pleasing and sensual rites and ceremonies. . . ." Many are led to those cults that practice free sex, chemical indulgence (alcohol, drugs), or other "free spirit" activities. This was most true in the sixties, but it has always been true to a large degree. [Of Superstition]

5. "If a new sect have not two properties, fear it not, for it will not spread. The one is the supplanting or the opposing of authority established, for nothing is more popular than that. The other is the giving license to pleasures and a voluptuous life." This is, of course, a key to our era as well as to many eras past (and future, no doubt). [Of Vicissitude of Things]

1525. If you don't dream about what you want to become, you will become what someone else dreams about for you. And as the saying is, "Your dream is my nightmare."

1526. Amazing Fact of the Universe #1: Every book, film, and song, no matter how vile or boring or silly or devoid of merit, has been pronounced by some critic, somewhere, to be a "masterpiece."

1527. When you make your choice, if you don't care about the cost, you can't object to the bill.

1528. "Some things are just meant to be." Why the desire to rely on fate, destiny, predestination? First, such a belief absolves us of the burden of analysis and choice. We need not ask whether this is the right person or action or alternative; we just accept it as predetermined. No thinking necessary. Second, such a belief relieves us of moral responsibility for the nature and consequences of the act. "That's illegal and immoral? Well, but it was destiny."

1529. "The smell of money attracts men just as the smell of

blood attracts a wild animal." — Gertrude Mathews Shelby

Men can smell money just as a shark can smell blood, and a similar frenzy results when they get close to the prey.

1530. Information is not merely presented; it is packaged. Clever and artful packaging greatly enhances the credibility of information, and those who know how to package are those whose ideas persuade. The packaging arts include the right kinds of details, attributions to or associations with seemingly credible sources, connection to other accepted ideas, the use of pictures that supposedly illustrate or show the truth of the idea, and so on. (Many a TV news story shows background or stock footage to illustrate it — for example, a story on ulcers shows people eating. This is visual "proof" of the facts of the story.)

1531. The more we do, the more restless, shallow, distracted, and unfulfilled we become. Choice soon becomes clutter. Thus the saying: do less; live more.

1532. Having more choices doesn't mean more happiness. More choices means more things we want to do. When we have many things to do, we become interested in shortcuts, so that they all can get done. We want the shortcut to love, the shortcut to health, the shortcut to wisdom — so our lives become shallower.

[July 30, 1995]

1533. Many people oppose a new idea not on the basis of some reason or principle, but because their imagination is too small.

1534. "Who runs this place, anyway?"

"No one runs this place. They walk it. This place is relentlessly pedestrian."

1535. "I'm not a bad person, I've just made some bad choices."

"You are what you choose. For each person is the sum of his choices."

1536. "Mediocrity knows nothing higher than itself; but talent instantly recognizes genius." — Arthur Conan Doyle, in *The Valley of Fear*

1537. Conclusion from reading a book about murder: most people are killed by their friends.

[Sept. 11, 1995; age 44]

1538. A plan without a budget and a deadline is merely wishful thinking.

1539. We pass through life believing that we are judging and measuring the events of the world, when in truth, the events of the world are judging and measuring us.

1540. "I've never seen a shred of evidence for the existence of God." One response might be that belief in God is an ontological choice that need not be defended by any evidence. One may say that God provides the most complete and rational explanation for all the phenomena of existence — not just the physical world, but the moral, esthetic, and spiritual world. Another response might be that those who see no evidence are really not looking or are forcing their perceptions — for who cannot see the evidences of design in nature, beauty, love, spiritual hunger, the question of first causes, and other "small but infinite" hints?

1541. Famous Last Scenes Dept. This man dropped dead in the middle of an argument over a piece of gristle in his steak.

1542. "What metaphor would you use to describe yourself as a manager?"
    "A fountain that waters the flowers at its feet."
    "And what metaphor do you think your employees agreed was the most suitable for you?"
    "Um, probably a yellow brick road."

"Nope."
"So tell me."
"You wouldn't like it."
"So they said I'm a wall, eh?"
"No, they said you're a deaf slug."

1543. Is a reason given for an action or belief an *ex post facto* creation (that is, a rationalization of emotional response) or a belatedly articulated rational source of the emotion? Is it pre-verbal thought, eventually verbalized as it comes into consciousness?

1544. People unsure of their identity use products to help define themselves. Marketers help by ascribing meaning (status, power, personality) to their products. For example, when a man buys a car, he buys a story he can tell himself about himself.

1545. "One man has the mystery of the universe and one man has the mystery of novelty. It is the latter that entertains us most."
— From a dream, the night of Sept. 23-24, 1995

1546. Of the things you want, which are possible? Of the things you seek far away, which are right next to you?

1547. Historically, value structures have been, by their nature, strict, absolutist, often intolerant. Literature often supplied a corrective to the rigidity, excess, the thoughtless conformity, the bigotry that resulted from such structures by subverting them. Now, however, prevailing value structures are loose, tentative, amorphous, even incoherent rather than strong and well defined. But contemporary literature is still playing the subversive. We now have subversion as a corrective to nothing—or moral tepidity at best—rather than as a corrective to a substantial power.

1548. "Isn't she beautiful?"
"Yes, but she's seventy percent water and twenty-two per-

cent fat."

1549. The difference between a slogan and an idea.

1550. The difference between a wanderer and a searcher.

1551. As life gets ever busier and we have less and less time for true learning and reflection — reading good books, thinking about ideas and their implications, we try increasingly to live and learn by ever more complex structures, schemes, and formulas: how to write, think, judge, grow wise, run a business, take part in a marriage. We have Seven Habits of, Ten Secrets of, Four Styles or Types, or Modes, or Levels of. We try to teach writing by recipe instead of by letting students read a few hundred books — because no one reads a few hundred books anymore.

1552. In any arena of decision making, including love, money, and software, the more options we have, the less committed we are likely to be to any one of them, because the more the options, the more likely we are to doubt the correctness of our choice. That's why large generations marry later and divorce sooner than small generations.

1553. **Lessons from the O. J. Simpson Trial.**
  1. Trust is more important than evidence. If someone doesn't trust you, your evidence is wasted, superfluous, invisible.
  2. The less educated a society, the less just it is.
  3. Critical to good thinking is the ability to construct hierarchies of significance. "This is important, but that is more important."

1554. Meaning is a product of thought. Therefore, to the extent we spend less and less time thinking, our lives become less and less meaningful. Thus, the busiest people are in the most danger of living meaningless lives.

1555. Lessons from Comdex in Las Vegas, 1995.

1. Las Vegas is usually thought of as the city built on the exaggeration of the dark side of humanity — greed, lust, excess, self-indulgence and folly — and indeed it is all these. But it is also a monument to hope, where thousands, in the face of loss, failure, and disappointment, continue to hope that the next coin, the next roll, the next spin, will produce wealth or at least a modicum of success. What a testimony to the resiliency of the spirit regardless of negative experience.

2. Appearances are important — but let's have some content and functionality, too. Software that just looks good has limited value.

3. One question we need to ask ourselves regularly when we are about to act: where did I get these values? Too often we act from motives or values we've adopted thoughtlessly by imitation or osmosis, without realizing that a little thought would cause us to act differently, or at least recognize that the values we are about to act in accord with run contrary to other values we consciously hold as part of our core.

1556. Do bad and dysfunctional people really believe that their way of life is the best way, the best set of choices, to bring them as close to happiness as they can get, given their circumstances and liabilities?

1557. To whom are books of wisdom addressed? Who reads them? The already wise? The would-be wise? How many of the would-be wise are there in the world? Do they change their lives for the better as a result of having read some pointed wisdom? Do the few who read and improve themselves have any effect on civilization or on the happiness of the world? Good ideas have always been around, so why don't they prosper or influence others? And what, in fact, is it that causes society to change direction — to get better, or worse?

1558. In a youth-oriented culture, increasing age means increasing decrepitude and marginalization. In a culture that respects the old, increasing age means increasing wisdom and knowledge.

1559. We are imitating ourselves because we don't have time to *be* ourselves.

1560. Why are so many creative people loners? Because creativity must be permitted before it can live. And it must first come to life before it can flourish. "Share your dreams." You must first have a dream before you can share it. You must be allowed to dream before you can have one. To speak a dream lets it breathe, to share a dream gives it wings. So why are so many creative people loners? Because creativity unlinks the chain, it lifts the wheel out of the rut, it suggests change, and change is greeted with fear and hostility.

1561. Do people apply to their own lives the philosophy they enjoy pronouncing to others? "Do as they say and not as they do" — that's not a very new piece of advice. So the problem is an old one, after all.

1562. The clichés of discourse make it possible to talk at length without the necessity of communicating. Words of supposed profundity are often at the bottom merely agreeably vague.

1563. Why do some unhappy people make choices that cannot possibly bring them happiness — choices that will clearly lead to more sorrow? Are they blind? No. They know. They prefer change not so that they will be happy, but so that they can be unhappy in a different way. Those in pain, physical or emotional, after a long irritation, come to believe that they could bear the pain better if it were felt somewhere — anywhere — else.

1564. Decision fear. Many people willingly remain indecisive, confused, noncommittal to another person or to an idea (like the faith) because they fear that to make a decision will cause them to lose freedom. The more choices, the more fear to decide, because the greater chance of being wrong. Thus, the more choices, the greater the paralysis. However, there are equal options among many choices, so that there is not just one right answer or even one best answer. And every decision is enabling as well as restricting. And lastly, if a decision is not made in a timely way, it will often be made by default. If you can't decide where to go this summer and summer passes, you've made a decision not to take a vacation, whether you wanted that decision or not. Similarly, you can't stay single and young indefinitely, waiting to find the perfect spouse.

1565. Words don't have the respect they used to. They are not as carefully chosen nor as carefully listened to as before. They are read hastily, shouted over loud music, spoken without thought, interrupted without care.

1566. It used to be that when people pushed the boundaries they did so because they believed that beyond the boundaries lay something good, something better than what was within the previous limits. Now most people seem to want to go beyond just to go beyond. They just want to sneer at the concept of limits, and maybe feel the pleasure of shocking others. But these days, there isn't much that's shocking anymore. The sacred and the private have been pretty much stomped into the ground. And Hollywood has treated us to just about every evil, whether violent or perverted or both, that a host of creative talents could invent.

[January 22, 1996; age 45]

1567. The selling process has made many people suspicious of relationships because salesmen create false relationships in order to manipulate people. A friendly overture is viewed with suspicion because so many times the friendliness is a cynical ploy. More and more we resist the demand for quick decisions because the selling process has taught us that quick decisions are frequently regretted. "Decide now, because if you have time to think, you will decide against the product." To be honest in our evangelism, then, we should not imitate the "buy now" tactics of many salesmen, lest we should seem to be peddling snake oil also.

1568. A lasting decision needs to be a rational decision with emotional agreement. The decision must make sense and feel right. Decisions required on short notice ("buy now") tend to be neither.

1569. The medium may or may not by itself be the message, but it is certainly the signifier, the purport, the embodiment of authority (or lack thereof). Newspapers and magazines are disposable; so too, by extension, are their ideas. What's seen on TV or heard on the radio is forgettable, because there is never any tangible presence to the information. Only an attitude remains. But what is printed in a book takes on a solidity, an endurance, a timelessness, a ponderous importance. How you read this thought—in electronic form, in a magazine, or in a book—will determine how profound you find it.

1570. Not those with the best information, but those who can tell the best story, are the ones who persuade us. This is not good.

1571. Spiritual battles are intellectual battles. Faith transcends reason but does not contradict reason.

1572. "Only the rock knows the heart of the tree." This is a proverb about friendship and about perseverance and patience.

1573. Few things create as much resentment as the feeling that one has been deceived. That is why people who find themselves enlightened or disabused about someone or something often become the most ardent enemies of that person or thing. And that is why the recognition of deception ends relationships so quickly.

1574. "Americans like to recast their social problems as technological ones, on which science and capital can be brought to bear." — Thomas Hine, *The Total Package*

But whether we are trying to conquer litter, AIDS, or educational underperformance, social problems are not amenable to technological solutions.

1575. Much modern rhetoric revolves around a simple change in terms. We wouldn't want to say that "order is bad," so we change "order" to "restraint," and say that "restraint is bad," which is much more attractive. Similarly, we wouldn't want to say, "Licentiousness is good," so we change "licentiousness" to "personal freedom" or "self expression," and then "self expression is good," rolls right off the tongue. Thus, we change "lust" to "stirrings of the soul" and debauchery becomes a spiritual act.

1576. We all like to see our ideas put into effect, because that makes us feel both creative and powerful. This is true even for little ideas, like, "Let's go for dessert and coffee." To acquiesce in such small matters is not trivial; it is an act of spiritual construction.

1577. "Why are people so thoughtless? Do they think they are going to live forever?" No, but they don't think they are going to die today, either. And that's enough to put off responsibility for one more day.

[April 20, 1996; age 45]

1578. Life is a series of unexpected turns. But we swerve most when we ask others to drive.

1579. Some things are done, not because they deserve achievement, but because someone has invested so much effort, time, or money that we would feel sad not to see it done. This is the sunk cost fallacy of human effort. However foolish the deed, we'd feel bad to say, "Stop now; you're wasting our time (and yours as well)." "I know you spent six hours getting this report ready, but we wanted only five minutes, and you've gone fifteen already. Please stop."

[September 21, 1996; age 45]

1580. Nothing is as resilient as a good idea.

1581. How you decide between trash and treasure shows who you are.

1582. A good idea has a hundred brothers. But to meet them, he must go out into the world.

1583. Words seldom come with a guarantee, but they are the longest lasting product we have.

1584. We are cast down when we focus on ourselves—what we can and cannot do or did or did not do. Let us focus on God and what he wants done and then trust his sovereignty.

1585. Suppose I show you a flurn, something you have never seen before. How will you know whether it is a good one or a bad one? You would have to ask, What are the goals of a flurn, and how well does this one meet them? What is its intended function and how well does it perform? (If you were more subtle, you might add indirect considerations such as environmental impact, general safety, and so forth.) You might ask about appearance, cost, durability, size, but this would imply a comparison to more than the goals of a flurn. You would want to know how it compares to other flurns. Hence the statement, "All judgment is by comparison." Our evaluations are either against standards (goals) or against similar items, or both.

[November 25, 1996; age 46]

1586. Lessons from Comdex 1996.

1. Communicate more by saying less. Dumping large quantities of information on someone in a short space of time is a waste. Teachers perhaps should take note of this.

2. The "free" syndrome, the scarcity principle, and human greed all conspire to make people take things they have no use for. Even when they recognize that something will be of no use to them, many people will take it anyway, simply because it is free.

3. Overheard boss bawling out employee: "Either you're part of the team or you ain't with us."

4. Overheard man in casino restroom: "I'm going to wash the bad luck off my hands."

5. After watching one man lose $1,000 on a single play at cards, the clanging of the nickel slots is less impressive.

6. In order for us to observe something, we must think about it. This is the difference between seeing and observing. It is possible to see a lot in a short space, but not possible to observe a lot in a short space. If you must cover a lot of ground quickly, take pictures, draw maps, take notes—and then later on, think about what you have seen. Otherwise, you have probably wasted your time. Take time to reflect and to analyze. Keep a diary of what you see, and in the process of writing, think. Thus will you truly observe.

7. Things I saw but didn't have time to observe: a leaky roof in a seven-month old casino, the whole city of Las Vegas from 1100 feet up, a bowling alley with 106 lanes, a bingo hall for 800 people.

8. On the street corners sleazy-looking men pass out pamphlets with half naked women in provocative poses. "Beautiful ladies?" the men ask. Beautiful, perhaps. Ladies, I don't think so.

[December 30, 1999; Age 49]

1587. Why are the supermarket tabloids so popular, with their obviously preposterous stories? Not so much because some people are appallingly gullible, but because information is now just another form of entertainment. Whether a story is true or not is no longer very important. The real issue is whether or not it is a good story. We have lost our love for truth because we have loved pleasure more.

1588. A principal irony of the information age is that we are too informed to be wise. We are too occupied with the ephemera of technofactoids, passing notions, and the always-changing news of the day (or minute). The huge quantity of information we must process daily prevents us from taking the time to be wise: to read, write, and think about values, principles, and priorities. We increasingly lack the circumspection that enables us to find value and meaning in our lives and their events. As a consequence, we pursue activity without meaning and live lives without examined purpose. The tragedy of info-fussiness was brought home to me when I recently noted that three years have passed without my having written down a single Glimmering. Where has my mind been? Processing information of little import in the long term.

1589. If we are forced by our occupation to face mountains of data glut, perhaps we can find wisdom there by analogy. I recently found an old notebook wherein I noted a couple of "metaphors from science to life." I quoted the following from *Machine Design* magazine: "Stabilization of magnets is possible because flux losses are noncumulative. Once the flux level of a magnet has been reduced by effects of a given strength, it cannot be reduced further by demagnetizing influences up to the same strength, and the magnet stays at a constant flux level." My comment in the margin was, "Building endurance or preparation through experience." If the behavior of magnets can tell us about ourselves, then perhaps we can find wisdom even in computer acronyms.

1590. A good imagination empowers practical accomplishment. We can accomplish more easily that which we can imagine first. Imagination prepares the mind for practical action.

1591. The most appealing bit of fakery is a seductive error mixed with some truth.

1592. The entertaining and the important tend to live at opposite ends of town. Thus, to emphasize entertainment values in education and religion depreciates their importance.

1593. **Lessons from the Consumer Electronics Show 2000, Las Vegas, Nevada.**

1. Even those trained in the laws of probability are willing to overlook what they know when even the smallest chance of an attractive gain is offered.

2. The chance to win a desirable prize at a definite later time tends to freeze ambition in the meantime, and all effort is suspended while the one obsessed waits for the time of the future possible win.

3. To see the face of greed, look no further than a buffet. All the insanity is there: lack of willingness to plan, seizing too much of what is first offered, overindulging to the point of personal pain. And the worst of it is that we can see the face of greed by looking in the mirror afterward, too.

4. The things we want we should want for a purpose, not merely out of a desire to possess. The world of marketing and social behavior has created a consumption compulsion in us that makes us want many things we have no use for.

5. Being creative is important, but not merely being creative. We have to apply it well. After all, substantial creativity goes into drug smuggling and slot machine design.

6. Who is fooled by the copycats of name-brand products? When you see an Olympia camera, do you think it is the same as an Olympus? Are Nokina and Nikon the same brand? Is Kingwood the famous stereo maker and not Kenwood? And if you buy Panashiba do you get the best of both Panasonic and

Toshiba? Is GVC just as good as JVC? Perhaps over the phone with a heavy accent, these names sound similar enough, but what is the result when the product is delivered?

7. Sign for Writing Pens: "Instruments of Distinction." Here, of course, "distinction" means "expensive." In a self-indulgent society that defines itself by consumerism and ownership, we distinguish ourselves with expensive possessions rather than by accomplishments.

8. In the race to possess and be "distinctive," practicality is not important. Witness the automobiles with so many speakers and amplifiers in them that there is no usable trunk space, the trunk must be opened to hear the music, there are no back seats (and in one car there was only the driver's seat).

9. Our dreams are our own. I may be sitting in a coffee shop dreaming of writing a book, while the person in the next booth is dreaming of adding several one-thousand-watt speakers and half a dozen amplifiers to his car.

10. The croupier at the craps table has several euphemisms for "You lost." When a player threw a five instead of a ten, the croupier said, "You're halfway there." After the player threw another losing number, the croupier said, "Your ten is overdue now."

1594. "She was a simple village woman." The person saying this was no doubt thinking about his computer or fax machine. Too often people confuse the possession of technology with being sophisticated. The village woman may have more insight into life and human nature than the speaker will ever utter into his wireless phone.

1595. Managers used to have signs on their desks or walls that said, "Think." Then they had signs reading, "Plan" or redundantly, "Plan Ahead." The sign we should all have in our offices today should say, "There are other choices." We are quite well aware that we have many choices, but we sometimes forget that our customers, friends, and colleagues have other choices—than us or our ideas.

1596. What does a candle gain by remaining unused, or lose by giving itself to light the world? (suggested by Marcus Aurelius, VIII.20.)

1597. Only by understanding the purpose of something (life itself, art, information) can we judge its value and success.

1598. The mind does not travel directly from problem to solution, but it nevertheless travels toward the goal. (Compare Marcus Aurelius, VIII.60.)

1599. Marcus Aurelius says that your soul is visible through your goals and your values (IX.34). No one, then, needs to bare his soul—we can already see it.

[March 10, 2001, Age 50]

1600. Wisdom cannot form merely in the interstices of busyness.

[November 2, 2001, Age 51]

1601. One of the hallmarks of pseudosophistication is mistaking criticism for analysis. Many journalists and even professors are so negative for this reason. They think that by criticizing an action or idea, they have demonstrated their superior intellects.

1602. Smart, smooth, and plausible—even persuasive—doesn't make it true.

1603. An idea dressed up in forceful, clear rhetoric, supplied with anecdotes and believable examples, seems worthy of belief. But it may be simply an information performance that does not describe the real world, the true situation, after all.

1604. We argue sometimes from plausibility to plausibility because we cannot argue from truth to truth (which the postmodernists deny anyway) or fact to fact.

1605. Facts are like rocks: Someone must tell their story before they have meaning.

1606. Saying no when you should have said yes can result in a missed opportunity. Saying yes when you should have said no can result in a wrecked life. So we are torn between the fears of being too cautious and being too impulsive.

1607. We say it's a shame that people base decisions on emotion or impulse rather than reason. But the reality is that they base decisions on social cues, peer pressure, cultural practices, and paths of least resistance—and not even on their own emotional preferences.

1608. **Lessons from Comdex, 2001.**
   1. At a secondary entrance to the convention hall, long lines of people waited to get past security as personnel used wands on almost everyone and asked most people to empty their pockets before passing through the metal detectors. At the main entrance, several security people waved everyone through their stations, even though nearly every person set off the alarm in the metal detector. To paraphrase Forrest Gump, "Security is as security does."
   2. At the DoCoMo exhibit, the promoters included four attractive young women wearing tight, brown leather dresses. Nearby stood a convention security guard, cap in hand, leaning on a vertical support, watching them closely. If anyone attempted to kidnap one of those young women, he was ready.
   3. The Airstik 2000 computer game joysticks use the same accelerometers designed to trigger automobile air bags in a crash. You never know when your role in the world will be to save a life or help a kid play.
   4. A young woman with a microphone at one exhibit stood hawking some product or other. Around the exhibit were several televisions displaying her presentation as she spoke. It was

somewhat unnerving to realize that she appeared more "real" on television than up there live on stage. On stage, she wore heavy makeup and was overlit. On television, she looked normal. We look to television to define reality for us. If it is on television, it really happened.

5. What captures your attention? As I walked down the aisle, on my left was Vivastar, whose company was being promoted by a large-breasted blonde in a silver jumpsuit. On my right was LG, whose company was being promoted by twenty-foot high twin waterfalls cascading over mirrors.

6. The clichés of fake friendship. The salespeople nearly all used the same opening lines: "Where are you from?" and "Are you here for the show?" This latter question is glaringly inane since we are standing at a booth inside the show when it is asked.

7. Always read the information tag all the way to the end. "This bottle of Aqua Fina is provided as a service for our guests. If consumed, a $4.00 charge will be billed to your room."

8. The Monte Carlo is a contrarian hotel. It has a 13th floor. You can go directly from the parking garage to the check-in and then directly to the elevators all without having to pass through the casino.

9. Beware the slippery slope of incrementalization. Play the penny slots, then the nickel slots, the quarter, dollar. Now you're hooked.

10. The company that gave away free pens that do not work properly. Tell me, what is the message that sends?

11. One set of quarter slots allowed the gambler to bet up to 25 coins at a time. You think you're playing a quarter slot, but you're really playing a six-dollar slot.

12. Buildings—or the Web—will attract students. The University of Nevada at Las Vegas reference librarian told us that traffic to the library increased three-fold when the new library opened in January of 2001. The 20,000 students use the library at a rate of 128,000 per month.

1609. The story of oxygen. It's okay to buy emergency oxygen for your boat, so I buy a couple of tanks for my mom. The dealer discovers I am a regular customer and says, "Next time you must have a prescription to get oxygen." A year later anyone can get five minutes of oxygen for $7 for frivolous consumption at an oxygen bar. Sure, if you want oxygen you'll likely never use for an emergency, or if you want some for entertainment, here you go. But if you want some that will actually help someone in need, show me a prescription.

1610. What amazes me is not the level of debauchery people indulge in, but the relish they display when bragging about it to other people. (Suggested by hearing a grocery checker announce, "I've never been to Las Vegas sober.")

1611. Expectations should be raised only to the degree they are likely to be met. Raising them beyond the probability of fulfillment results only in frustration and disappointment.

1612. That guy's so deep you'd need a quarter-inch ruler to get to the bottom of him.

1613. The more you know, the better you can see.

1614. Many intellectuals are more interested in the image of being intellectual than they are of ideas, truth, or thinking.

1615. Many academics have so much learning that they don't know anything.

1616. The speed of change forces us too often to make today's decision based on yesterday's knowledge.

1617. One of the sadder aspects of life is that we spend most of our time and energy on the production of ephemera and only stolen moments on what might endure.

1618. We sometimes hear the comment on an idea or belief that it "defies logic." What does that mean? It means that to the commentator, the idea does not appear to be logical. Therein lies an issue in itself. But even if we grant the commentator's viewpoint, what we have is simply an idea that is not logical under current assumptions. And the assumptions are often where the problem lies. Think of the inventors whose ideas "defied logic" but later became brilliant successes.

And logical consistency itself is not a badge of truth or rightness. Schizophrenics are extremely logical people, but their beliefs are all wrong:

"Why are you wearing aluminum foil on your head?"

"To block the electric zapper rays."

"Who is zapping you?"

"The CIA."

"Why would the CIA want to zap you?"

"Because I know secret information they don't want revealed."

And so it goes, for as many questions as you can ask.

1619. Everyone believes much more than he can prove. Whether philosophers or scientists, all make use of inferences, inductive leaps, rational conclusions, logical deduction, a priori assumptions, ontological foundations, and so on, to construct their view of what is true and real.

1620. Our assumptions are based on our own experience. The narrower our experience, the narrower our assumptions.

1621. The warmest answer I ever received when asking a girl to lunch was, "Oh, I'd love to!" The coldest answer was, "Why?" Fortunately, that page of my life has turned.

1622. Why is it that children's fiction commonly expresses moral values and judgments while adult fiction does not? Adults are not ready to face moral instruction, while children are eager to find values. Is it too much pride? "Don't preach to me."

1623. There is a crucial difference between available information and information actually in play. If the information exists but is not present in the minds of the problem solvers or decision makers, it may as well not exist. The entire field of knowledge management is built on this fact. The need for greater cooperation among police agencies is also relevant. If one agency knows a fact about a suspect that it does not share with another, the other is disadvantaged in its work.

1624. **Lessons from reading *Blaze: The Forensics of Fire*.**

1. It's rare to have a coincidence. Two crime scenes with similar factors are likely to be linked. A third example means that there is no coincidence. (Compare not just arson, but anthrax letters, and some air crashes such as the DC-10 cargo door problems.)

2. When people stick by a lie long enough, they actually begin to believe it. A criminal may eventually believe he is innocent.

3. The first activity after a sudden input of information (seeing smoke, hearing an explosion, seeing someone running, and so on) is conceptualization. We need to make sense of the scene, to answer the question, "What's going on?" Until that question is answered, we cannot proceed. Cognitive stabilization is required before any further steps. The next step is to answer the decision-making question, "What should I do?" Finally, we must implement the decision and act. There is no surprise, then, in watching people react slowly if by that we mean that they delay acting when they witness or are involved in an impending disaster. Every emergency requires conceptualization first and then a decision. These processes take longer in some people than in others. In emergencies, the information is often ambiguous and uncertain, so there is no wonder that the processes take even longer. Problem solving is similar. Given the answer to the question, "What happened?" or "What's wrong?" or "Who did this?" conceptualization sets up multiple hypotheses and pursues them. Decision making asks, "What should be done?" as in, "Who is guilty?" or "What was the cause of the accident?"

4. People pattern their behavior on the basis of a script that suits their personality and the location and event. (Spectator, diner, driver, romancer, etc.) Even in an emergency, people are reluctant to change this pattern (see page 150).

5. In fires, "people don't panic" Rather, "it's lack of panic, if anything, that kills people" (pp. 164-65).

[March 4, 2002, Age 51]

1625. Lessons learned from reading *Air Disasters*:

1. Some facts gathered during an investigation will confuse rather than clarify the issue. Bad weather, a common cause of an air crash, may mislead investigators when it is present but not a factor in a crash.

2. A pattern is not recognizable until sufficient instances are available. A single accident (or crime) sets no pattern. A second one may raise suspicion, but often has enough differences to mask a pattern. A third, perhaps. A fourth, probably a pattern. A fifth, definitely. How soon do you decide you are looking at connected events (same defect or same criminal)? Three is usually the minimum.

3. Human factors includes more than just the ability to conceptualize a problem or operate an aircraft competently. It includes sociology as well. How well do the crew members work with each other? For example, is the captain an arrogant, self assured type who thinks he can do no wrong and will not listen to his first officer telling him to pull up or change course? Or is the first officer overly deferential and unwilling to tell him that the captain has made a mistake?

1626. Traditional ways persist long after the reason for them has ended. Operatic singing style, that unnatural, shrieking warble, began as a means of producing enough singing volume for a large audience. The style is pre-technology. It is less natural and less beautiful than a softer voice, but it was necessary in the era before electronic amplification was available. Now it is an unnecessary artifact that could be dispensed with. However, the style is so deeply ingrained by now that we instantly recognize it as the "high singing style of opera." We may even describe it as beautiful. Musicals written since amplification became available do not use that style.

1627. **Points of interest from** *Photo Fakery*.

1. Those models in fashion magazines are not only idealized perfect specimens, but they are not even real. Computer surgery has enhanced every feature and removed every defect.

2. There are two types of false captioning. One, the staged photograph with a real or implied caption that misleads the viewer. Two, a caption that falsely describes the content of an ambiguous photograph. Does this photograph of people sitting on the ground depict prisoners or resting travelers? Many photographs need explanation. How accurate is the explanation?

3. To spot a faked photograph, "It is also necessary to employ a higher level of analysis than that of the originators" (63). The analyst must think beyond the details the faker thought to take care of.

4. The desire to believe something makes it more credible (compare hoaxes of any kind). Families of lost soldiers in Vietnam were utterly convinced that faked photos showed their lost loved ones because the families wanted to believe the loved ones were alive. (See pp. 63-65, 94-95.)

5. A photograph may be completely unrelated to the story it illustrates. The viewer may understand the photograph to be evidence, proof, or at least an illustration (example) of the story, when, in fact, it is only a decoration. The photo may have been taken years earlier or in some far removed situation. (See 109.)

6. Instead of doctoring a photo, the scene itself may be faked, posed, or manipulated and then a "genuine" photograph taken. (Cf. Civil War photographers moving bodies around, pp. 30-35.) (See 111.)

7. Great example: "Lundahl always loved to tell the story that the British discovered a German decoy airfield in North Africa during World War II. They subsequently sent a lone bomber over the field, which dropped a wooden bomb" (120-

121).

8. Disinformation may have a short life and yet still be effective. A faked photo may be discovered within days, but it could still have a desired effect. For example, a faked photo put out a day or two before an election can cause a candidate to lose (127).

9. "Other than a fingerprint, the ear is the best human feature for making a positive identification of an individual" (154).

1628. One of the great disturbers of quiet in old age is the fear of losing competence. As people get older, they can't find the right word, can't play the piano as well, can't sing on key any longer, can't write. Those who used to climb on the roof to fix the antenna or crawl under the car to change the oil realize that the days of their vigor are over. Sometimes there is a desperate attempt to remain competent; otherwise, the aging person feels devalidated.

1629. Hasty generalization may be facilitated by the intensity of response. That is, one or two occurrences of an event that is striking in effect for a particular person will be construed as larger or more common than is actually the case. Three examples. (1) A reviewer of a book noted that the author "constantly" tells readers what they already know, pointing to a single example in a 180-page book. (2) A film reviewer says that an actress in a film wears a bikini "in practically every scene," when in fact she does so for only a few minutes out of the entire film. (3) A professor takes his class out for pizza once during the semester. Later he hears a student saying, "I liked the class because we were always going out for pizza." In each of these cases, the experience was so intense or remarkable for these people that they overgeneralized about the frequency of it. (It has been said that poor children draw coins as larger than they actually are.)

1630. Because examples are so powerful, what the world needs is better examples. Tell a story to prove a point. Tell a story to change a life. Or, in a less dramatic proverb, give an example to illustrate a concept. Bring your readers with you. Help them understand in concrete terms.

1631. A hundred threads make a rope. Though each thread is weak by itself, together they are strong. A single piece of evidence may not by itself prove anything, but a hundred pieces all pointing in the same direction make a convincing argument.

1632. From *The Book of One Hundred Lies:*
     33. It's plug and play. It installs itself.

1633. The decision process is always time limited. The amount of time available for a decision should always be taken into account both before and after the decision. More time often means a better quality decision. Con artists and high-pressure salesmen attempt to limit the decision time so that full reflection is not possible. Even sales ("Limited time only," "While supplies last," "Sale ends soon") often attempt to force a quick decision in order to prevent full reflection.

1634. All married people know that they will eventually be parted from their spouse by death. The only question is when.

1635. That which has no name cannot be discussed. To talk about something, it must first have a name. Putting a name on a new idea is a powerful act, for the idea can then be discussed.

1636. The slogan, "Benefits and Discounts if you join the club," also means, "Penalties and Upcharges if you don't join the club."

1637. The young believe too much, and the old believe too little.

1638. The skeptics are not really interested in truth, lest truth should lead them to God. What they are really interested in is enough of a reason to cling to their preferred beliefs so that they can feel at peace with themselves.

1639. Every time they fit in a new piece, often after removing three other pieces, they congratulate themselves on having completed the puzzle. They never think, "Perhaps we are wrong about this, too, just as we were wrong before." Nor do they think, "We still see only part of the total picture. We might be misinterpreting this." The less information they have, the more dogmatic they are about it.

1640. It was easier for people to worship God in past ages because they assumed that God was higher they were and his ways higher than their ways. God, they believed, knew more than they did. Now many people seem to think they know more than God and that God is their equal, or almost their equal. They feel free to criticize his works, his actions, his values, his rules, even his motivations.

1641. We insist that things must be comprehensible to us by our own rules. If we don't understand something, we say, "That makes no sense," and reject it, not thinking that it may be greater than our capacity to fathom. We should say instead, "I cannot understand this," but then we would have to be humble enough to think that.

1642. That we cannot discern a purpose behind an event does not mean that there is none. We are unaware of the world's purposes much of the time. Why then do we question God's purposes?

1643. Those who fear an idea seek to control it and make it safe for themselves by defining it in personally acceptable ways.

1644. The world wants to feel sophisticated without going through the mental effort needed to become sophisticated. The penalty for indulging this delusion is money. Pseudosophistication is expensive.

1645. Mental illness is an argument against monism. The brain is ill, which confuses the mind, but the mind is still there. The personality and the person are still inside somewhere, fighting the brain to come through and to grasp the world and experience.

1646. Imagination either reduces or enlarges. It enlarges when a girl screams at seeing a tiny bug and fears being hurt by it. It reduces when men dare to criticize God. See Pascal, 138 MT, 77-78.

1647. Advertising's four appeals are fear, pride, sex, and greed.

1648. Kindness is more important than generosity.

1649. Postmodernism is an information pinball game, where you bounce from belief to belief, none true, but it doesn't matter because in the end you're dead. Game over.

1650. If your mind is not listening, your ears will hear nothing. If you are not ready to hear, you will not understand. If you are not ready to understand, you will not hear. A book of wisdom is lost on those not prepared to be wise. "They hear but they do not understand."

1651. Writing creates a permanence in a world of change. Good writing preserves forever the wise thought, the beautiful image, the new insight. And it can be shared with others a hundred or a thousand years later. Writing comes as close to touching Forever as we on earth can get.

1652. Writing can't be taught, but it can be learned. — Proverb.

1653. Writing is an esthetic object and can be an object of beauty, feeling, and intelligence.

1654. When someone judges something, he does so not only by reference to the thing being judged, but "according to the sort of person that he is at the time" (Pascal 1). Judgment is the matching or corresponding of value to the object or event. Therefore, not only do you judge an object or event, but it judges you. How or where something appears on a scale reveals the scale itself.

1655. Are they against authority because they are against God, or are they against God because they are against authority?

1656. Is art *dulce et utile* now? No. *Utile* means didactic which means oppressive imposition of personal values which means authority which is bad. Okay, so is art only *dulce*, only entertainment? No different from fluff? No, it has powerful personal visions of the artist in it. Is some art better than other art? If so, there must be standards of judgment. If not, we are reduced to solipsism, whimsy, arbitrariness. The rejection of authority is everywhere, except in evolutionary dogma. Values clarification, nothing is evil or wrong, only "personally or socially unacceptable" or "socially sanctioned."

1657. **Socrates Reads a Poem.**
    "Here, Socrates, read my poem and tell me how good it is."
    "How can I know if your poem is good or not?"
    "If you like it."
    "It has no metaphors, so I don't like it."
    "But you're trying to force it into the rigid structures of the past and place antiquated demands on it."
    "Well, what are you trying to do with your poem?"
    "Express myself, my feelings."
    "But I can't detect any feelings here. Does that mean that I as a reader have failed or that you as a poet have failed?"
    "I don't care whether you can detect my feelings or not."
    "Then why did you write the poem?"
    "To express myself."
    "To yourself? You are the only audience?"

"Maybe."

"So poetry is no longer the public medium it used to be. Well, then, tell me. Does your poem, in your mind, succeed well in expressing yourself to yourself?"

"Yes."

"Then, by your standards, this is a successful poem. The only remaining question is this. Why did you ask me to read it? If it is a poem written to yourself, why show it to me?"

"I wanted to know what you think."

"To me, the poem says nothing and does not even say that well. In fact, I'm not sure why you call this a poem. It seems rather to be awkward prose broken into arbitrary, short lines. Why did you break a sentence up into short lines rather than just write it out?"

"Because it's a poem. Duh."

"Tell me. How many drafts of this poem did you write?"

"Just one. It flowed directly out. The 'spontaneous overflow' thing, you know. I just wrote it down."

"So you created a work of art in twenty seconds. My, that is an accomplishment. How long do you think it will last?"

"I don't care."

"Do you put no value on your art?"

"All my friends like it."

1658. If you're good looking, the locks will fall off.

[March 17, 2003; age 52]

1659. God is as deep as you want to go.

1660. God gives us the sour grapes, too. He doesn't expect us to say they are sweet.

1661. To prevent plagiarism, an ounce of instruction is worth a pound of punishment.

1662. When arguing against a project they oppose, they seem to argue from the assumption that a good project should be without cost, without risk, and without tradeoffs. But when they argue in favor of their own plan, then the ends justify the means, success should be pursued "by any means necessary," and "no cost is too great."

1663. Wouldn't billions of years of decay have turned the earth into talcum powder?

1664. Stupidity is one thing, but stupidity at high volume is something else.

1665. Good is not only better than evil, but good is smarter than evil. Evil prospers by denying, transgressing, loosening boundaries or rules. Thus, evil has no compass and no anchor. Without compass or anchor, evil cannot make quality decisions, for there are no standards, no wisdom. Good decisions come from comparison and judgment against standards. Moreover, evil has to use censorship, political correctness, fear, power, information control, lying, propaganda, and brainwashing in order to advance itself. Anything but reasoned argument, where it will lose.
  (Cf. T. S. Eliot on liberalism, that it is a loosening, moral entropy, a winding down.)

[August 25, 2003; age 52]

1666. People like stories because we live by analogy. We learn by hearing and reading about the experiences of others. Experience connects to experience much more immediately and powerfully than idea connects to idea.

1667. The declared strength, cogency, and persuasiveness of an argument depends in part on the attractiveness of its conclusion to those assessing it. For example, Hume's attack on miracles or criticism of the argument from design. Some prefer these arguments to be convincing and call them "devastating" while others view them as unconvincing. "Definitive" is sometimes a matter of personal bias.

1668. The argument of intense, personal, real-time, three dimensional experience is difficult to refute.

1669. Tangibility is a powerful defeater of philosophical deduction.

1670. Thus, the argument from design will always be with us and always be powerful, regardless of the attacks of clever philosophy (even when disguised as science).

[March 1, 2004; age 53]

1671. The easiest way to deprive people of freedom is not to enslave them forcefully, but to change the definition of what freedom means.

1672. "If you love those who love you, what credit is that to you? For even sinners love those who love them." — Luke 6:32
     But we often don't even love those who love us, so we aren't even as good as sinners.

1673. It is essential to talk about important truths and beliefs, whether or not you have new ideas or fresh arguments for them. What is not discussed seems not to exist, or at least not to matter. Every generation is alike eager for ideas and ignorant of truth. If truth is not continuously proclaimed, it will be buried by the errors always being shouted by the culture.

[January 4, 2005; age 54]

1674. Isn't it odd that so many people act as if sin is no big deal and yet they are confused and shocked by how much pain and misery there is in life?

1675. When people refuse to accept any authority other than facts, then various authorities will be reframed in the guise of facts.

1676. Lessons from visiting Las Vegas for the Consumer Electronics Show, 2005.

1. I am still struck by the women I see in Las Vegas. So many of the women in their 20s, here apparently with their boyfriends or just a male friend, have a peculiar, almost unique expression on their faces. It appears to be a combination of the thought, "I know I'm doing something wrong," and the thought, "I'm being mature and liberated and sophisticated and modern." I'm not sure they really believe the latter thought, since the look shows much more determination than cheerfulness. They are determined to believe that they are showing their individuality and independence, by an act of will. They seem to be using this determination to overcome embarrassment or even "guilty knowledge." They often have a look that seems to say, "I hope I don't see anyone I know." The men they are with seem happier, more confident, a bit cocky, often more animated.

Many of the women in their 30s and 40s, especially the employees, have a very hard and even cold expression that seems to say, "I can't be tricked again." They look as if they have been betrayed in life too many times and now they are angry about it.

Most of the foreign (Hispanic and oriental) women workers and tourists, especially those in their 50s, are very friendly.

The expressions on the faces of the scantily clad women (in showgirl costumes) on the various posters advertising shows reveal few if any genuine smiles. Usually the faces have a cynical, sour, or even bored expression.

All told, I'd guesstimate that only about half the women I saw appeared at all happy. On the way out of town, a billboard asks, "Was it worth it?" Good question. (Then the billboard adds, "God cares." Hope that message sticks.)

2. The new monorail is a testimony to bad design. You'd think that in the 21st century, the nuances of great design would

have been worked out long ago, considering how many years ago Disneyland built a monorail and how many years buses and subway cars have been built and improved. But no. The Las Vegas monorail is pathetic. The track is often bumpy. The train speeds up and slows down abruptly like a bus in city traffic. Half the time the train creeps along, and sometimes it just sits at the station for a long time, doors open. The handrails are too far near the edge of the cars and thus unreachable by those standing in the center of the cars, who need them most. There is no handrail above the doors. There are too few seats. Rider traffic flow is such that caution tape and extra employees are needed to tell people where to load and when. The monorail stations are difficult to locate from inside the hotels (placed in back with few directional signs). The station at the convention center doesn't even connect to the building. Riders must walk outside, down an escalator, and across traffic lanes to get to the convention center. Ticketing and using the ticket in the turnstiles seems more complicated than necessary. The system is only months old and yet it has broken down repeatedly and parts have even fallen off the trains.

3. Gluttony is partly a product of temptation. Kings may have been fat in the past because they were offered twenty things to eat at each meal and wanted to sample all of them. Hence, buffets tempt us — me successfully — into overeating. It's not the "get my money's worth" idea after all. We simply do not manage choice well. Maybe this explains the promiscuity of handsome boys and beautiful girls.

4. The lure of gambling is that it combines hope with greed.

1677. Truth never asks whether or not you like it, whereas falsehood always aims to please.

1678. The choice and dominance of a worldview has less to do with its truth content or explanatory power than it does with social and economic advantage. How well it caters to personal autonomy is a large factor, too.

1679. "God never wastes a hurt if we let him write our story."
—Steve Saint

1680. Sacrifice does not involve a calculation of efficiency.

1681. Most people willingly read philosophy only when it is disguised as a story. Or better, we prefer that the medicine of philosophy be mixed with the honey of narrative. One to another, grandson to grandfather, daughter to father, woman to woman, those around a campfire—they all say, "Tell me a story." They never say, "Let's discuss philosophy," or "Tell me some timeless truths," or "Quote a few proverbs of wisdom." I guess that means they won't say, "Let's read a few Glimmerings," either.

1682. Three Latin mottoes:
   Fides et Veritas (Faith and Truth)
   Credo ut Intelligam (I believe in order to know)
   Cogito ergo Credo (I think; therefore, I believe)

1683. Insight is power. When you learn how to reframe a situation in a way that gives you new hope for resolving an ongoing problem, you feel powerful and confident. You were hopelessly stuck in a corner, but now here is a doorway.

1684. Feeling that we are the only person with a given problem is debilitating. And the converse is true too. When we learn that our problem is actually quite common, we feel better. For some reason, knowing that we and our problems are part of the "normal" human experience makes us feel less isolated and hopeless. We still may not solve the problem, but we feel akin to mankind. Sharing our problems, even in simple discussion, helps us cope.

1685. May your words always have meaning and your deeds always have purpose.

1686. Americans are encouraged not to take their religion seriously, especially when it might interfere with what are now deemed secular concerns (such as a store being closed on Sunday or the influence of religious teachings on public policy). And, of course, we'd never want our faith to get in the way of our desire for pleasure or consumption or practical activity.

1687. **Thoughts on the fact that an evil novel has sold 25 million copies while mine could not even find an agent.**
    1. Evil pays better than good in this world.
    2. Evil is better connected in the information environment than is righteousness.
    3. There's less of a market for moral fiction, because morality implies restraint.

1688. My newest personal verse is John 15:16: "I chose you to go and bear fruit—fruit that will last."

1689. A book provides us with a two-dimensional experience, while life itself is a three dimensional experience. Sometimes, however, that missing dimension is a blessing and we feel much safer with the book experience.

1690. Horror Stories of the Pampered Life. Chapter 16: Three Days Without Flossing.

1691. "How would you explain the work of the Holy Spirit?"
    "The wind that fills the sails that drive the boat."
    "The battery that lights the bulb."
    "The blanket that wraps our lives in joy on a cold night."
    "The whisper at the interface between sound and thought."
    "The light that shows the mind its path through the brain."

1692. Help me to use your property well, O Lord.

1693. How do we experience faith? How should we experience faith? Should we be intellectual or emotional? Is Christianity an emotional experience? Worship and music are emotional. But what about the truth and value content? Those must be processed and responded to with both heart and mind. And a third possibility: Faith is experienced in activity. "Show me your faith through your deeds." She said, "I love you so much," and betrayed him. Was this faith or faithlessness?

1694. Wisdom cries out at the beach;
       She speaks loudly at Starbucks;
       At the theater exits she raises her voice;
       "How long will it be before you empty heads get a clue?
       How long will you dis the truth and hate knowing who you are?"
                              — Proverbs 1:20-22 (Doax version)

1695. "But for this purpose I came to this hour." —John 12:27. And we all want an easy, trouble-free life.

1696. Many people like emotional experiences for their own sake. Men and women alike enjoy horror movies (being scared), roller coaster rides (being thrilled), and other adrenaline pumping activities (white water rafting, driving fast). One difference between the sexes is that many women also enjoy feeling sad, or at least emotional in a way akin to sorrow. Hence, the romance novel, and the whole concept of the "good cry." Maybe Aristotle was right about catharsis. Men, though, tend not to understand why women like to feel sad vicariously.

[June 30, 2005; age 54]

1697. Your life is subject to change without notice.

[December 11, 2005; age 55]

1698. Sin is a lot more understandable once you've been around the block. It's still not pretty or approvable, but where you once might have said, "How could anyone do that?" you now say, "There but for the grace of God go I."

[September 1, 2006; age 55]

1699. Things move so fast these days we move from anticipation to nostalgia in the time it takes to glance at our wristwatch.

1700. The trouble with people is not that they want to be happy, but that they want to be happy by their own rules. The real rules of happiness — the only rules that work — simply don't appeal to them. And what are those? They involve a considerable amount of kindness, generosity, compassion, and deference. Less, not Ish. Selflessness, not selfishness.

1701. The ocean says, "I am constant, I am patient, and I will win."

[September 24, 2007; age 56]

1702. Youth is about experience; maturity is about meaning.

1703. Even if there were a shortcut to wisdom, and you put it on sale for half off, many people wouldn't buy it because they know that wisdom would always be disagreeing with the advice of their hormones.

1704. Some people could find the cracked tile in any mansion.

[November 26, 2009; age 59]

1705. My question to every married woman in America is, "Why did you marry a man who is always wrong about everything?"

1706. A woman gets married so she will have someone handy to criticize.

1707. If God doesn't exist, you don't exist, either. If there is no spiritual reality, then there is no *you* in that body. Your so-called thoughts and words are just the product of the random or deterministic electrochemical activity of the three pounds of wrinkled meat inside your skull.

1708. A Short Dialog
"If God exists, why is there evil?"
"Are you asking because you really want to know, or because you want to score debating points with your own negative arguments?"
"I really want to know."
"And this is an important question for you?"
"Yes, very."
"That's good. That means that you have been thinking about it. What research and answers have you found so far?"

1709. As many apologists have pointed out, the argument from evil is not an argument against the existence of God and for atheism. It could be an argument against the existence of the Christian God, but not an argument against any god. What about Zeus (Jove) and the Greek and Roman pantheon, where the gods were selfish, cruel, and exploitative toward humans? Or what about a bad god?
It has also been pointed out that if God doesn't exist, then evil doesn't exist, either, because without a divine, objective standard against which to measure actions and events, none can be objectively called evil. Without God, we have only personal opinion, cultural norms, and social consensus, all variable and subject to change.

1710. Yes, pride is the problem, all right. You have to answer. You have to correct. You must show you are right. You have to assert yourself. After all, you don't want to be a doormat. What about your wants? Why just go along?

Samuel Johnson once said, "There is, indeed, nothing that so much seduces reason from vigilance, as the thought of passing life with an amiable woman." Next time you have a minute, look up the word *amiable*.

1711. How much would you pay to make your spouse happy? Or rather, how much would you pay to avoid destroying your spouse's happiness? A dollar? Ten? More?

There once was a wife who told her husband, "You use too much shampoo. I have longer hair and I use less than you do." Now, the shampoo the man used cost about a dollar a bottle (he was a thrifty sort), and he got perhaps 100 shampoos out of a bottle, which is a penny a shampoo. If he reduced his use in half, he would save half a cent. He didn't. But every day for years afterward, when he took a shower and shampooed his hair, he remembered his wife's criticism. Thus, his wife destroyed his happiness for half a cent.

1712. It's about control. There is no rational basis for criticizing a spouse over tiny, insignificant things, such as how you dry your hands, how you take the lint out of the dryer, or how much shampoo you use. What exactly is the purpose of criticism like this? Are you trying to make your spouse happier?

1713. Some of us are insufficiently grateful to God because we have been raised in an environment where everything was always there. We've always had the refrigerator, the microwave, the cell phone, the washer and dryer, electric lighting, hot and cold water on tap, drains, thermostatically controlled heating and cooling, you name it. Some people (please not me) need to be put in the desert with nothing but a plastic fork for three or four days. On their return, perhaps they would know gratitude. A "vacation" to the slums of India might be salutary, too.

1714. Whenever a narrower epistemology encounters a broader epistemology, the narrower one will declare the broader one irrational. The broader epistemology contains truth claims that are unintelligible to the narrower philosophy because they cannot be understood by the narrower one's inadequate premises.

[August 1, 2010; age 59]

1715. You never know when you're going to find concrete in a tree. The truth of this improbable statement was made manifest a couple of weeks ago when I was sawing up a dead avocado tree. I came to a particularly tough spot where the chain saw would go no farther. Upon investigation I noticed that a hollow spot in the trunk had been filled with concrete as a sort of patch. My chainsaw blade was ruined. But I did remember that I was the culprit who had filled the hollow trunk section many years ago.

1716. Some people just want to feel normal—so they do whatever they see their friends doing. They will do nothing if their friends aren't doing anything; and they will commit every manner of stupidity and criminality if their friends are, all just to fit in and feel like one of the members of the team.

1717. Some people will do anything to be famous or rich or both. But some people will do anything for the mere hope or distant prospect of being rich or famous or both. The latter are often assisted in realizing their dreams by a group of selfless philanthropists known as con artists.

1718. The lies are in the adjectives. That's the most amazing statement of phenomenal truth. What a shocking idea.

1719. "How was your date?" "Remember what I said about that Southwest chicken wrap I had at the coffee shop the other day? It was okay, but I'd never order it again."

1720. The first effort to oppose an idea is to kill it aggressively, to oppose it vociferously. Thus we have seen "the death of God," the end of truth, "beyond freedom and dignity," and so on. There is suppression of evidence, lying, distortion, but at bottom rebuttal and heated argument. "Truth does not exist."

The second effort to oppose an idea is to ridicule it. "Who can refute a sneer?" it has been said. Make fun of it, pretend that only the naïve or bumpkinish can believe it. "Truth? What a quaint idea. Did you get it from your mommy?"

The third effort to oppose an idea is to redefine it and the terms surrounding it. God is whom you make him, morality is a negotiated agreement that permits individual impulses to be permitted, tolerance is approval of those with alternate life-styles. "Truth is merely personal opinion."

The fourth effort to oppose an idea is to dilute it. Christian belief is mixed with the beliefs of other religions, formerly as-tute interpretations of a literary text are mixed with postmod-ernist multi-meanings. "That statement is one truth, of course. But also true is its opposite. And true also are many other mean-ings."

1721. Where truth is solipsistic, power becomes the universal authority. When absolutes are denied, only power is left for universal compliance.

1722. Given how many revolutions in theory and perspective there have been, it's odd that the current generation of scientists cannot see that their theories do not necessarily describe reality accurately or give insight into the true nature of things. During every age, the reigning theoretical constructs are held with vi-cious commitment. I recall how vociferously continental drift was ridiculed before it became dogma. Phlogiston was proved to be true until it wasn't.

1723. How disappointing to discover that someone with a spe-cial talent—his gift of knowledge or ability—simply cannot ex-plain how he does what he does.

[February 9, 2011; Age 60]

1724. Lessons of the Consumer Electronics Show, 2011
1. Keep track of your notes. I recorded half a dozen pieces of wisdom learned from the show and then proceeded to lose the notes.

1725. "The central work of life is interpretation." — Proverb
And the central error of life is extrapolation.

1726. Which statement will the average man never hear his wife or girlfriend say to him?
A. I went to a 50% off shoe sale, but I didn't buy anything.
B. Sure, I'll be glad to go to Home Depot with you.
C. Look at the girl over there. Isn't she cute?
D. You are absolutely right. I agree with you completely.

1727. The evolutionists stress structural similarity to argue for common ancestry. That's because the real challenge — what they can't explain — is the complexity of the *processes* involved in life. Metamorphosis of caterpillar into a butterfly is dramatically complex and of "irreducible complexity" as the intelligent design folks say. Operations in the cell — the processes of life — present inexplicable levels of interactivity. So all the evolutionary folks can say is, "Well, this animal looks a lot like that one."

1728. *Now faith is the assurance of things hoped for, the conviction of things not seen. . . . By faith we understand that the universe was created by the word of God, so that what is seen was not made out of things that are visible.* — Heb 11:1, 3 (ESV)
"Faith is the evidence of things not seen."
God has permitted us to see some things but we don't know what of the creation he has not (yet) permitted us to see. It was thought for awhile that the colors of flowers were to attract pollinating insects like bees. Then it was discovered that bees see infrared images and not colors. God has permitted us to see the color image but not the infrared, until he allowed us to see it through technology. What other aspects of flowers do we still not see?

Until powerful telescopes were invented, the distant galaxies looked like clouds of gas. Now they are seen as stars. God has permitted us to see these new stars and the greater expanse of the universe. What do we still not see?

Operations of the cell we can now see well, but there is likely more. What is the smallest particle? It used to be an atom, then protons, then subatomic particles like quarks, then on down, down, down, to something like an idea behind all matter.

Oh, the depth of the riches and wisdom and knowledge of God! How unsearchable are his judgments and how inscrutable his ways!
—Romans 11:33 (ESV)

For his invisible attributes, namely, his eternal power and divine nature, have been clearly perceived, ever since the creation of the world, in the things that have been made. — Romans 1:20 (ESV)

"Oh the depth of the riches . . . of God" was written when men had only their bare unaided eyes to see. God had not yet permitted them to see deeper, and yet even then his "divine nature" was "clearly perceived" in his creation.

What will we see when God allows us to see everything he has made to its fullest extent (in the kingdom of Heaven)?

And what is to come on earth? Who knows, who can imagine what beauty lies in the creation that we just can't yet see? It's like a geode—a plain, gray, ugly rock on the outside, but inside filled with beautiful crystals—who could imagine it?

[June 5, 2011; Age 60]

1729. To the question, "Where is wisdom to be found?" the answer is, It's not what you look at, but what you see; it's not what you listen to, but what you hear; it's not what you read, but what you understand. It follows, then, that it's not what you know, but what you live.

1730. "Let's throw away the compass," they said, "because we don't like the direction it's pointing."

1731. Which is more important: What you do or who you are? Answer: What you do is who you are. Counter Answer: What you do is less important than Why you do it.

1732. The biggest mistake liars make is not that they can't remember which lie they told to whom. The biggest mistake is their failure to realize that everyone knows they are liars.

1733. The central error of life is extrapolation. Too often we generalize from one occurrence, one example, one fact, one impression. We allow our imagination to fly immediately beyond modest and blushing probability into fantastical and sneering improbability. Then follows the reification of imagination — from fantasized, to possible, to probable, to fact.

1734. Relativism's final victory will be the elimination of judgment in every arena. Judgment is already gone in art, and in most morality. Judgment depends on standards, which depend on universal truth, which implies God. And we can't have God. But without judgment, there is only the dictate of power.

1735. Spiritual battles are fought in part with intellectual weapons. "You shall know the truth."

1736. The R's of Relationship are Religion, Rest, Reading, Repast, and Romance. Pray together, nap together, read together, eat together, and love together.

1737. I was in an undergraduate course on drama during the late 60s and early 70s, where we were reading one of those popularly anthologized plays—a Shakespeare, Ibsen, maybe Chekov. After a small amount of discussion in the class, a Hispanic student remarked, "I can't relate to this. It's not about my people or my experience." Forty years later, I now have a response:
- That's exactly why you should be reading and studying the play. It will broaden your horizons, give you a big-

ger context for life, show you what you can aspire to, what there is beyond your limited life experience.

- It really is about you, because human nature does not change. The surrounding cultural situation may change, but we all have similarities in longings and aspirations, the need for love and relationship and so on.
- Here's an opportunity to learn about others who are not like you and who do not share your culture.
- You will be working and living with others, so here is an opportunity to learn about them.
- The culture of the others might just be the culture of the power brokers of society, and if you learn how to operate successfully in their culture, you have a chance for betterment by working with the power brokers of society.

1738. Postmodernism has encouraged the idea that all interpretations are equally valid and that if someone says, "That's how I feel" or "That's my opinion," then no one can object—because how can you disagree with someone's feelings? The way around this seeming impasse is to ask for some specific passage or statement in the book that has produced this feeling. If the person says, "It just is," or "That's just how I feel," ask if someone else can identify a passage that might suggest those feelings.

The goal of analysis is to draw evidence-based conclusions, to give reasonable interpretations that lead to understanding and perhaps even wisdom.

1739. When people are unwilling or afraid to engage an idea they disagree with, they sometimes keep away from it by leaping to a wild and extreme caricature of the idea—much like satire. For example:

"Jane, you seem so negative in our meetings."

"Oh, so you want me to be a Pollyanna doormat and agree with everything anyone says."

Or:

"Look at this roadside trash. I guess the penalty for littering is not strong enough."

"Oh, so you want the death penalty for everyone who accidentally drops a gum wrapper."

1740. Usually we want our experiences to have meaning. We look for the meaning in or behind everything we experience. But then sometimes — and more often for some people than others — the experience *is* the meaning. The experience (say, swimming with dolphins) is meaningful because it creates a positive memory, a good feeling that can be recalled later. When ancient folks tell the stories of their lives, they usually narrate events in simple terms and seldom draw a moral from the account. For them in old age, the experience was the meaning.

1741. One writer, John Horgan, has called the theory of multiple universes "science fiction with equations." That description covers a lot of "science."

1742. We should always distinguish between a logical explanation with evidence and a plausible explanation with rhetoric. Rhetorical explanations build bridges between the extant and the imaginary.

1743. We love our friends because they are like us. And we love our friends because they are not like us.

1744. We credit our tools for events we have accomplished with them. "My sword won that battle." "My hammer built that dog house." God works through tools — us — but the credit goes to God for completing the action. "The maker of all things is God."

1745. "The pipe is only inches underground, we have examined every joint and there are no leaks, and yet the pipe is leaking profusely."

"But professor, that makes no sense."

"That's exactly why it's so interesting."

1746. Ask the same question of several people until you get a consistent, coherent answer. Then ask someone else to verify it.

1747. Sex on the brain at a computer show: Product representatives wearing double-entendre T-shirts: "I'm easy" and "Want to hook up?" Product representative in a knit dress and not wearing underwear. Dancer in fishnet stockings. Who says high tech isn't sexy?

1748. Why is everyone in a hurry? They are afraid they will miss something. But enjoyment, understanding, wisdom, knowledge, relaxation—all will be missed by hurry.

1749. They live their lives in hours and days, not in years and decades. They don't look beyond tomorrow, yet they believe they will live forever—and be always young. The longest commitment they can make is a couple of years to a wireless phone plan.

1750. Why is knowledge important? We live according to what we know. Where do we get the knowledge that guides our lives? TV, film, stories, academia, textbooks, popular books, the Internet. Where *should* we get knowledge? The Bible, good books, accurate knowledge and wisdom, good stories—true to human nature.

1751. And now the bad news. People do not change their beliefs as a result of reason, argument, evidence, or thinking, but because of stories that resonate with them. Why anecdotal evidence is so powerful, the availability bias, the recency bias—all the things decision makers warn against—are the very things that persuade people. That's why fiction (novels, short stories, film, television, music videos) is so important. Fiction is a worldview shaper. Stories shape worldview, and worldview shapes—nay, becomes—civilization.

Thus, a false and harmful worldview, promoted by a novel or film, can permeate an entire culture.

1752. As you know, fact claims that fail to cohere with our plausibility structures are denied ontological status.

1753. You sit down at McDonald's and begin to eat your egg McMuffin. A stranger sits beside you, drinking a coffee and eating something. He seems to notice that you are reading *The Practice of the Presence of God* by Brother Lawrence. He says nothing, and after five or ten minutes, he leaves. Was this a chance encounter? A random event? Or are the events that we call chance, accident, random, really God's appointments that we don't understand yet — if ever? Was a seed planted or watered?

Even in secular thinking, is chance really a name for an extremely complex cause and effect that we cannot understand?

Those who analyze traffic "accidents" discover the chains of causation, the matrices of causation that resulted in the event. They don't use words like *chance* or *random*.

1754. In most cases, mockery is a sign of ignorance, for it betrays a lack of understanding. We make fun of those things (and people) we don't understand or can't comprehend. The greatly uneducated are sometimes fond of ridiculing academics (not that many of them don't deserve ridicule) because the uneducated have little concept of abstract thinking.

1755. **How to corrupt a culture.**

1. Use counterfeit reason. Arguments that seem to make sense but that are distorted or rely on subtly false premises can lead even the thoughtful astray.

2. Desensitize people to error or even evil by claiming that the error is actually truth and then by constant repetition of that claim. Remind people of it, urge them to believe it, recommend it to them. Present it in terms of fairness, liberation, tolerance, justice or any other valued abstraction. Soon we will look less

unfavorably on it, then we will become neutral, then favorable, and finally promoters.

3. Remember the availability bias. If you promote the corrupt idea or its acceptability everywhere and always, it becomes the first thing people think of.

4. By a constant drumbeat from everywhere, the idea can exploit the recency bias also.

5. Make it familiar. Dress it in "ordinary folks" style.

1756. To sell an idea, it need not be true or wise or good. It just needs to be familiar. Here's a story.

A man took over a failing restaurant only to discover that his inventory included several pallets of canned worms and only a few other staples. Worms were on the menu, but it didn't take the man long to discover that no one ordered them. Knowing he would go broke if he didn't clear his inventory and regain his investment capital, he started to offer worms.

"Would you like a side of worms with that burger?" he would ask.

The answer was always, "No, thanks."

Finally, as his rent was soon due, he got an idea. Every time a customer ordered something, the man offered worms.

"Do you want baked potato or worms with your steak?"

"Would you like stuffing or worms with your turkey?"

"Would you like fries or worms with your burger?"

Occasional customers always chose the usual side, as did regular customers—for a while. But in the face of constant offering, many of the regulars began to think that maybe a side of worms would be interesting to try. The idea of eating worms as a side dish became so familiar to them that it no longer seemed repulsive or even unusual.

1757. Belief: commitment to the truth of an idea.

Truth: conformance to reality.

Knowledge: properly justified, true belief

Faith: confidence of belief, sustained in the absence of full knowledge.

1758. Pride. Pride leads one to a sense of self importance, leads to arrogance, self righteousness, indignation at any perceived affront, overbearing, controlling, need to argue to win, need to be right all the time. In a marriage Pride causes misery for both partners.

1759. Truth must be lived to have value.

1760. Faith: confidence in the truth of something not proven.

1761. Comment on reading about yet another person raised by strict, Christian fundamentalist parents, only to rebel and fall away from the faith. Why do seemingly so many parents use Christianity as a control mechanism and why do they make Christianity out to be all about No?

1762. Once upon a time a famous actor delivered some brilliant lines in a play. What he said was wise, witty, exact, powerful. Audiences were amazed. He was asked to appear on a TV interview.

"Tell us about your success with this play," the interviewer said.

"Well, I, um, acting, you know. It's, like, I, well, I'm an actor, and like that."

"Yes, of course. But how is it you are so perfect a hero, always coming up with exactly the right thing to say and the right thing to do?"

"I act like, you know, there's people and there's people and I'm an actor, and so forth."

>> There is a better Writer for our lives than ourselves. We should follow his script.

1763. Knowledge begins with faith, for unless you have faith (trust, belief, trusting belief) in the person or book presenting the knowledge, you will not accept it and therefore will not learn. So the sequence is faith, knowledge, understanding.

[January 30, 2012; Age 61]

1764. Christians are hated by those whose ultimate values are power and control, because Christians have values and obedience to something beyond the earthly controls of power, money, prestige, and so forth. Someone who cannot be controlled by these things is someone to be feared and despised.

1765. The more tarted up the booth girls, the less they know about the product. If you want cute or sultry, take a look. If you want information about the product, ask one of the less attractive girls.

1766. A dog isn't greedy until he's given the opportunity.

1767. The sad thing about people passing out hooker cards on the streets of Las Vegas is not that they are a bunch of greasy, overweight short guys with untrimmed moustaches. No, it's that there are young women doing it—who must wonder how low they've sunk to be doing that.

1768. You begin to suspect you can discover personalities from facial expressions. Then you walk back past a girl who seemed fresh and wholesome when you looked into her face, only to see she has a tramp stamp.

1769. Life's little ironies. The hotel installs water-saving aerators and shower heads, but then you have to run the hot water full force or five or ten minutes before it gets warm enough to shower in.

1770. Why does it seem incongruous to see ordinary looking girls all tarted out? Does that mean we think it's okay or normal to see beautiful girls all tarted out?

1771. A million ideas competing for limited space.

1772. Thoughts from the Consumer Electronics Show, January 2012

What an experience means, if anything, depends on whether you have a conscious search for meaning while you are in the experience itself or when you thoughtfully reflect on it. If you merely enjoy it thoughtlessly as it occurs, you will not gain mentally from it. In your daily experience, ask, "Is this a parable? An analogy? An example of—?" Does it tell an exemplary story or cautionary tale?

1773. We sometimes transfer a mental model from one thing to another too casually. I had a travel pack of wet wipes and used the mental model that they are like Kleenex, and since I had put my Kleenex pack into my right back pocket, I put the wet wipes there too. At some point in the day I noticed that my pants were wet in the back. Sitting on a pack of wet wipes and sitting on a pack of Kleenex are not the same after all.

1774. Last year, you and your product had reached the forefront of innovation. You had a unique product that set you apart and created envy among the other manufacturers and inventors because they didn't think of it. You were a celebrity. This year, there are twelve other companies making essentially the same product, only better in many cases. You have been dismissed as an also ran. The news media no longer call.

1775. Even the most organized, well orchestrated, carefully structured and scheduled information set is likely to be experienced as a random diffusion of unrelated pieces because of the sheer quantity of information streaming and screaming around it. Only those who can orchestrate a disrandomification of their message set will be able to communicate coherently.

1776. Many people go through their lives waiting for something great to happen to them. Sometimes when they grow tired of waiting, they take foolish risks or make big mistakes in the form of seriously wrong choices.

1777. It would seem that Tradeshow Giveaway Theory 101 would teach that booth operators should plan to give away a certain number of freebies each day, and that if under this plan inventory began to run higher or lower than predicted, a suitable adjustment would be made. However, it was clear that in many cases, the booth operators had seen their inventory of giveaways grow larger than projected. But instead of adjusting their speed of giving, they just continued along the same model until an hour before the show was to end. Then, looking at the boxes and boxes of leftover freebies, they began a frenzied effort to give the items to anyone who wanted them. Take two or three, they would say. One generous man said that he figured out that shipping the freebies back to the home office to wait for another trade show would cost more than reordering new goodies later — it was cheaper just to give the stuff away. Others don't realize that they will have leftovers until the final end-of-show call. Then they look dumbfounded at their remaining inventory — now suddenly realizing that they could have given it all away.

1778. If the stream of experience is too fast, there is no time to reflect and find meaning. Thus is education much less powerful that you would otherwise think because education is in some sense compressed experience.

1779. Pattern lock occurs when you go thoughtlessly through life on automatic and don't stop to think that you are wasting time, taking the wrong approach, being burned out by the work environment. You need to adopt a predictive, calculated-pace judgment of what's important. Analyze your habits.

1780. Iceland has a large percentage of beautiful women because the Vikings captured the best looking women and brought them back to Iceland. Similarly, Las Vegas attracts beautiful women because there they can be paid for having only a tiny talent and lots of good looks. So they eventually marry and have children. This accounts for the disproportionate number of beautiful girls and women in the colleges.

1781. When we are faced with something new — really new — we use analogies, similes, and metaphors to clarify the new thing. But when the new thing does not suggest a mental model right away, we must construct our own. The danger in the second method is that we can just sit there. When no schema (mental model) comes to mind, we end in a near trance, mouth open, thinking, trying to find something that will explain the new object under consideration, but looking rather dumb.

1782. At a tradeshow, always ask, "What does it do?" or "What type of business does this product (and your booth) belong to?" Some people can't explain. You've heard the arrogant, condescending folks say, "I couldn't explain that in a way you could understand." The question here is, "Could they explain it in a way *they* could understand?"

1783. There is a love of acronyms. Don't believe me? Just sign this simple NDA and I'll tell you how I know.

1784. Attendees come to the learning conference and sessions with wild hopes for marvelous solutions — as promised by the session titles — "Wow Your Learners," "Create Amazing Training in Half the Time," "Ten Tips to Keep Every Learner Riveted to Your Course," only to find ordinary comments and platitudes, together with some mild ameliorations and remedies. No miracles. Mostly a lot of educational snake oil.

1785. Conceptual delay. When faced with something unfamiliar, many people stand idle uncomprehending, searching for a mental model or schema that they can attach to the thing to make it intelligible. They are frozen physically while their minds search for something relevant, some analogous thing. Similarly, when something occurs which is beyond one's ontological paradigm or plausibility structure, the result is to stand and stare and possibly deny the reality of the input from one's senses. The less familiar the experience, the longer the time needed for conceptualization and hence understanding and acceptance. Compare the disciples' reactions to Jesus calming the storm.

1786. **Evidence of a bankrupt ideology:**

1. The ideas are held dogmatically, even irrationally.

2. Opponents' positions are distorted, even falsified. Much use of the straw man.

3. Opponents are attacked constantly as knuckle-dragging cretins. Much use of ad hominem and personal attack.

4. Opponents are not permitted to present their philosophy or arguments or evidence, nor even their responses to the ideologues' attacks. The ideologues who control the media — broadcast and print — and the educational institutions — school boards and university departments — suppress the opposition's ideas and arguments, even to the point of going to court to sue to suppress them.

5. At least some of the ideologues admit that their dogma or ideology is more important than strict, empirical truth.

Now look at the promoters of Darwin, Marx, and Freud.

1787. If you make a mistake when you're working with 10,000 volts, you won't learn anything. — But your buddies will.

1788. When you begin to measure the success of your day by how many green lights you make on the way to work, it's time to change jobs.

1789. Locked into a worldview. To a fish in a pond full of algae, the sun is green. The fish sees the thin, gentle water plants waving in the water and cannot conceive of an oak tree that does not bend. Experience makes the fish suspicious of any reasons or even evidence that conflict with its beliefs. The fish is immersed in a worldview that colors its thought and experience. Its interpretations are shaped by the surroundings. The other fish share the fish's environment and therefore its worldview. The fish reinforce each other. When the duck puts its head under water and tells the fish that the sun is yellow and that oak trees are real, they ridicule the duck and swim away.

1790. Young people dating or even just hanging out try to impress each other with their conversation. Once they stop trying to impress each other, a real relationship can begin. (And, of course, if they never stop trying to impress each other, a phony relationship becomes permanent.) Impressive stories, an air of sophistication, exaggerated mannerisms to oversignal interest in the other person—that is, nodding, talking rapidly, gesturing, constantly looking into the other person's eyes—all these things signal keen interest, whether sincere or not.

1791. The pomos like to tell personal narratives that provide anecdotal evidence for their points, because they know that their listener can't challenge a personal story as to factual accuracy. The result is a kind of historical revisionism, an embellishment and even a fabrication of life stories that always seem to be making a pro-Marxist point. Compare *I, Rigoberta*, a book filled with fabrications (that just happen to paint the class struggle and oppression by the running dogs of capitalism), yet told as a personal narrative of an indigenous poor woman.

1792. Darwinism is a secular religious cult, of a particular kind—utopianism. Utopianist cults exhibit the following characteristics:

1. Furious intolerance of any and all opposition, questioning, or criticism. Opponents are unqualified, their arguments and evidence are not science, etc.

2. Obsessive focus on the enemy, and criticism of opponents' position, to the detriment of providing positive support for their own position.

3. Hierarchical, led by a priesthood of wise scientists.

4. Hope in the earthly perfectibility of mankind, because of the belief that human nature is pliable.

5. Monopolistic and totalitarian, fearful of competition, intolerant of dissent, attempting not only to suppress but to punish all opposition.

6. Instead of engaging opponents with counterarguments, attack them with ridicule, sneering, and an attitude that they are beneath contempt; punish them with job loss; use the courts to prevent them from presenting their case.

1793. How the Princess Used Quantum Mechanics to Find Her True Love. A story in the modern kind.

1794. Events with highly complex causation might appear to be random because we cannot (yet) identify their causes. Causation matrices and chains of causation can be difficult or impossible to populate. Suppose Cause A causes Cause B which results in Effect X. If Causes A and B are 10 years apart, how easily can the chain be forged? And if Effect X is 100 years after Cause B, how will we connect Cause B to Effect X? In other words, what we call chance might actually be a highly complex chain or matrix of causation. Chance is what we call it in our arrogant ignorance.

1795. Keep an eye on your brain.

1796. Defining guilt away. Want to escape the guilt of shirking responsibility or just plain doing bad things? Your choices are: (1) Disconnect cause and effect. (2) Redefine guilt. (3) Redirect all blame to others. (4) Deny free will and blame determinism.

1797. If you have to pull rank, you have failed as a leader.

1798. Some people are afraid to think outside the box, as the cliché has it. Others are so box-oriented that they want to close the box itself and let no new idea in. Examples of their responses to suggested solutions:

- We wouldn't ever need that.
- Let's not add things.
- I doubt we'd need that.
- Let's stick with what we have.
- We've already completed our report (idea, system, solution, study).
- Let's not get carried away.
- This is quite sufficient for our purposes.
- We can't afford to get too radical here.

1799. Isn't it interesting how the ideas pressed forth from the media, the academy, and the philosophers are all in the direction of a flight from meaning? Determinism, the illusion of choice, chaos theory (in some writers' interpretation), materialism, naturalism, postmodernism. The flight from meaning is the freedom from meaning, because it leads to the freedom from responsibility, and that entails the freedom from guilt. So no more do they have to admit they will pay for their own sins when they reject God. They ask, "What sins?"

1800. Perhaps we have no free will after all. Determinism is true and choice is an illusion. In that case, I have no choice but to reject that idea. I'm fated not to believe in determinism. So don't argue with me. It's all predestined, foreordained. You have the opposite deterministic belief? Guess that makes us two blocks of concrete facing each other.

1801. Some philosophers are now saying that what we see in the natural world is randomness masquerading as order. However, that is only the view from one standpoint. I would claim that what we see more often than not in the natural world is order masquerading as randomness. There is intelligent design behind "chance" or "randomness." The fact that we cannot now at this moment explain how any of these mechanisms really works is not an argument for its falseness.

So the attempt to explain away a Designer of the universe could backfire, because the attempt to explain away a Designer by an appeal to randomness might just stimulate the search for and discovery of very complex design.

1802. Love is an action for the benefit of another. For example, Jesus gave himself as a gift to us, so that we could live.

1803. Many knowledge claims include a pronounced emotional investment that far exceeds the sample owner's stakes. In other words, if the claim is wrong, the plan loses money.

Even when the claim is clearly wrong, the consequences minor, yet the adherents behave as if processing it is a matter of life and death. I just plan to bring a hunting bear.

[Author's note: I have left this Glimmering just as it was written, so that it might serve as a cautionary example against writing late in the night when I am falling asleep at the keyboard. Evidently my brain falls asleep before my fingers do.]

1804. Liberalism, like its undiluted relative communism, is not about fairness or equality. It's about power and control. Power to impose a utopian vision on others "by any means necessary." After all, those who know the truth better than the blind masses need the power to impose that vision on everyone—for everyone's own good.

1805. Many people are in love with error and falsehood because they enjoy their sins and at the same time cognitive dissonance pressures them to stop feeling bad about their behavior. So they excuse their sins. But they go further. They call their sins *good.*

But they are so in love with sin and the false that they cannot allow others to disagree with them. Others must agree that the false is true, and if not, the falsehood lovers will hate them—and call them evil.

Yes, they are so committed to the advancement of darkness under the name of light that they will persecute and punish those who disagree. This is the power of ideology. No more of this, "I disagree but I will defend your right to say it," stuff. Now it's, "I disagree and therefore you are evil and I will do everything in my power to silence you and suppress you and harm you."

[August 29, 2012; age 61]

1806. Your team reads your actions more carefully than they read your emails or your memos.

1807. Those who have given up moral absolutes and Christian faith have also given up the concept of guilt. All that's left is personal and corporate shaming of those who make a mistake.

1808. Leadership is five percent talk and ninety-five percent modeling.

1809. "I've told you a million times, stop exaggerating."

1810. Why do people put up with psychotic leaders so often and for so long? Think about it: Nero, Caligula, Hitler, Vlad the Impaler, Saddam Hussein. And on a smaller level, cult leaders like Jim Jones and Charles Manson. It's because people like the charismatic, confident person who can provide them with order and structure, so they don't have to make decisions for themselves. (For decision making is both a joy and a burden. We want to be autonomous in theory, but in practice we like to be shown the path. See 1 Samuel 8:6: "Give us a king.") And power in a man is an aphrodisiac for women and for men a source of hope for gain from the powerful.

1811. The goal of narration is to immerse your reader emotionally and intellectually in the experiences you are describing through the language. That is, you must create a simulation of real experience using only words. The goal is to enable your reader not just to understand what you are saying but to experience reality only by reading your words—to see the events and feel the emotions you describe.

1812. Pain reveals the allegiance of your heart. When suffering comes, you either trust God or you don't.

1813. The media and academe join together to decide what they will mock and scorn and call false or shameful. And they agree on what to promote or worship. Thus, on the one hand there is a consensus of intolerance and on the other a consensus of exaltation.

1814. The checkout stand cashier jobs are filled with pretty girls without a path, waiting to be led astray by a good looking, smooth talker. They think that opportunity is knocking — and it is — but they don't realize just whose opportunity it is.

1815. **Games they play at work.**
    1. Let's throw someone under the bus.
    2. Let's disrespect whoever is absent.
    3. The Hot Potato Blame Game.
    4. Hunt for the Guilty, Punishment of the Innocent.
    5. Pass off the work.
    6. Tell a preposterous lie in a meeting and ask a coworker to confirm it.
    7. Pay lip service to corporate values, modern leadership practices, and collaborative decision making, then use command and control management. Oh, and call disagreement "insubordination."

1816. Good looking young women in their twenties who allow themselves to be led astray by good looking young men often become bitter, hostile women in their thirties. The lesson they got from being used and abused is not that shortcuts eventually lead you to dead ends. Instead, their conclusion is that men are pond scum. And they are angry about it. That's not what the fairy tale books said.

1817. It's really hard to find truth when you don't believe it exists. Not many people look for something they think isn't real.

It's even more difficult to find truth when you don't want it to exist and when you are afraid of it.

1818. The more knowledge we attain, the more difficult it is to think objectively, purely, clearly. We have developed so many assumptions, givens, shortcuts, thought habits, and epistemic filters that when we encounter a new idea or an unexpected knowledge claim, we recoil if it doesn't fit our set of boxes, ruts, and scripts.

1819. **Scarecrow.** noun. Extreme exaggeration of another's assertion, produced in order to avoid the need for thoughtful engagement with the idea.
Example 1:
"You know, it might be a good idea for you to compromise once in awhile and go along with the group."
"Oh, so now I'm supposed to agree with everything anyone says, and just be a doormat and let everybody walk all over me."
Example 2:
"I read an article claiming that most research findings are false."
"Oh, so science is just make believe and nothing is true."
Example 3:
"I find the evidence for Darwinism unconvincing."
"Of course. And the Earth is flat, and space aliens built the pyramids, too."
The Scarecrow turns a stated idea into an easy target—a straw man—and recoils from it with anger and loathing. It's a way to reject an idea that the listener finds threatening.

1820. In the disparity between expectation and reality, disappointment is not a problem of what actually occurs (reality) as we usually think. Disappointment is a problem of expectation. Disappointment is a form of resentment—anger that things did not match our requirements or beliefs. We are offended that reality did not perform according to what we thought—that is, what we assumed. Expectation is more than a hope, in fact, even more than an assumption; it is a presumption about the future, a presumption that reality will match (or live up to) our wishes and dreams.

Many marriages hit rough seas because the partners married their own imaginations, replete with a set of rigid expectations. These almost delusional views of the future create the tension and sometimes the battles, together with the resentment, over the mismatch between expectation and reality. Changing reality is a difficult remedy in these cases, because reality is under less control. Expectations can be controlled—and reduced—more easily. All this to say that one of the keys to happiness is to hope for more but expect less.

[January 1, 2013; Age 62]

1821. Somewhere in the Sherlock Holmes lore, Holmes tells Watson something like, "You look but you don't see," or maybe "You see, but you don't observe." The point is that you can take a look at something without really thinking about what you are seeing. Similarly, we can read something without understanding the words' implications for our lives. This is going through the motions of reading, not really reading. Bible reading can be this way, especially if you say, "I must read a chapter a day," and then rush through it so you can say you did it.

1822. Grandfather Solomon's Analogies, #1. When grandfather Solomon saw a young man using his cell phone to write an essay for his college class, he said, "You're trying to cut timber with a hacksaw, son. Get yourself a real tool and do the job right."

1823. The two purposes of wisdom are first, to use it and second, to share it with others.

1824. "Better is a cup of herbal tea where there is love than a filet mignon served with contempt." — Proverbs 15:17 (Doax Version)

1825. Proverbial wisdom ("Waste not, want not" for example) embodies a wealth of insight into the human condition, offering guidance for many situations. The challenge lies in the application. After all, some proverbs conflict with each other:

> *He who hesitates is lost.*
> *Look before you leap.*

Of its many definitions, perhaps the most helpful in this circumstance is that wisdom is appropriately applied knowledge. Proverbs form a set of tools, and wisdom is knowing which tool fits which situation. To have a variety tools from which to choose — screwdrivers, wrenches, files, pliers, drills — is the first step. Collect the wisdom of proverbs. And then learn how to apply them; learn which to use to support a decision in a specific situation.

Thus, instead of thinking, "Slotted screwdrivers conflict with Phillips screwdrivers," understand that each has its purpose.

1826. Catching up to Pascal. In his book, *How We Decide*, Jonah Lehrer says that our emotions "actually reflect an enormous amount of invisible analysis" (35), and so, "Our emotions are deeply empirical" (41). This means, he says, "The process of thinking requires feeling, for feelings are what let us understand all the information we can't directly comprehend" (26). Blaise Pascal in *Pensees* (1670) long ago remarked, "The heart has its reasons which are unknown to reason" (Lafuma 224). I was always puzzled by this, as well as Pascal's statement, "All our reasoning comes down to surrendering to feeling" (Lafuma 2). But now it seems to be clear: feeling or emotion is pre-verbal thought, brought to consciousness as reason.

Objection: Emotions can be deceiving. Answer: So can reason. Pascal notes that "reason can be manipulated in any way one pleases" (Lafuma 2). Listening to your heart and listening to reason both need to be done carefully and circumspectly.

1827. Grandfather Solomon's Analogies #2: Sometimes Grandfather Solomon gave good advice in an odd way. When he saw someone change from one task to another right in the middle, he would tell them, "Don't open a new can of worms until you've finished eating the first one."

1828. Truth has so fallen out of favor that many people are turning lying into an art. One technique is to accuse to excuse: Accuse others of lying so you can lie too, claiming the opposite. The two opposite claims confuse the situation, and if you're caught, use the excuse that your opponent is lying too. (Don't worry that the excuse is a tu quoque fallacy.)

Another technique is to create biased narratives—fictional history—that pretend to describe what is or was the case, when in fact they distort, misrepresent, or even imagine events. Shall we call this revisionism "fictory"?

1829. The saddest thing is not that people halfway destroy their lives by shortcutting. Taking shortcuts is infused throughout the culture now and few people seem to resist it. But the saddest thing is that, once they realize that taking shortcuts does not deliver the success or happiness they thought, these people double down and want to shortcut the shortcuts.

1830. Grandfather Solomon's Analogies #3. "You're asking a shoe salesman if you need new shoes."

1831. Another point made by Jonah Lehrer in *How We Decide* is that our brains contain circuitry that attempts to predict what will happen. This circuitry informs us about its predictions through our emotions—our hunches, our intuition. If you think about it, you can understand how prevalent a role these brain cells play in our thinking. Our biases, assumptions, prejudices, and expectations are all types of predictions about what will happen. So, what is the purpose of these cells? In a fast moving, complex world, where the situation needs to be conceptualized quickly, this predictive process serves to simplify things and offer us a quick insight into understanding what's going on. And, of course, there is—or would be—security in predicting the future, even a soon-to-come future. That's what keeps fortune tellers and horoscopes popular.

But our biases and prejudices, and to a lesser extent, our assumptions and expectations, are frequently more harmful than helpful. Our emotions and their intuitions can be helpful, but they are also often risky and unreliable.

1832. What ploy is more common than the artificial compromise ploy? You want 50 so you ask for 100 and then you compromise for 50. The consultant or veterinarian or automobile service writer wants to do three things and so he suggests five things you need. You compromise by eliminating two. The tree trimmer wants $700, so he quotes $1200 and compromises with you for $700. We all know this, and we all know that we are being exploited by the anchoring bias. Yet we continue to respond with evident content, as if we think we are getting a good deal, shrewd negotiators that we are.

1833. Remember that God made woman as a helper for man, not a do-everything for man.

1834. The Air Conditioner salesman.
"Before we get to the details, here are some numbers I just made up showing the approximate costs.
"Why should I choose your company?"
"Because five years ago, our competitor unknowingly sent a sex offender to a single woman's house."
"Your price seems high."
"Sign now without getting any other estimates to see if we're gouging you and we'll give you ten percent off. But you have to sign now."

"Isn't that a social manipulation technique known as the scarcity principle?"

"But who you gonna call? We fixed one woman's system that had been sitting without the final installation for three years. The installers suddenly demanded an extra three thousand dollars and when she refused to pay, they left in a hurry. Took her three years to win her lawsuit and after that she couldn't collect."

"I hope that's not common."

"Yeah? Well, a few years ago the authorities invited a bunch of companies to come out and check an air conditioner and 60 percent of them didn't even have a contractor's license. But we do."

"I'll have to be careful."

"Well, you don't even know who you are doing business with. These other companies use subcontractors to do the installing."

"And you don't?"

"Well, we use subcontractors to do the installing and the first year of maintenance, but after that it's our company's job to service your system."

"Hmm. I'll have to think about that."

"How does 18-month, zero percent financing sound?"

"Great. But that doesn't make the price any lower."

1835. They might be witty and clever, but using condescending characterizations of people ("poptarts") or things ("popera") is really a thinly disguised attempt at controlling conceptualization.

1836. Caulking, like lying, can cover a multitude of mistakes. But in neither case are the mistakes remedied. They hang around waiting to be exposed.

1837. I Remember High School. In high school, when a guy said, "She's stuck up," it probably meant, "She said No when I asked her out."

1838. Overheard at the High School reunion.

"Hey, Gloria. I remember you. You used to be cute."

"Oh, thanks, Tom. I remember you, too. You didn't used to be a jerk. Wait, I take that back. You were always a jerk."

1839. "Convenient" and "nearby" as in "convenient parking" or "restaurant nearby" shows how open to exaggeration, opinion, and different interpretation some of our humblest words can be.

1840. Think about a restaurant sign that says, "Yifeng's Authentic Mexican Food." Why is that funny? Why does it seem ironic? Can't a person of Chinese heritage cook authentic Mexican food as well as anyone else? As well as a Mexican? Our laughter reveals a prejudice — a stereotype — lurking in our unconscious.

1841. **The results of Free.**

1. Free is a greed amplifier. When something is free, you want more. How much free is enough?

2. Free manipulates buyers by letting them think they are getting a bargain. Instead of "Receiver and speakers, $2000," it's "Receiver, $2000. Show special, free speakers with purchase of receiver."

3. Free is bait for later spending. "First month free." "Sign up now and get a free movie."

4. Free means prepaid by others. Someone needs to cover the cost of anything free.

1842. **Lessons from the Consumer Electronics Show 2013, Las Vegas, Nevada**

1. The uncontrolled greed for a plate towering with crab legs at a buffet reveals how weak and shallow are human self-restraint and consideration for others when opportunity is at hand.

2. I love the way Asians hand things — business cards or small gifts — with both hands to the recipient. It reveals a graciousness missing from most Americans these days.

3. Too cheap a bag with the company logo will be swallowed by a better bag as soon as it is seen, and the cheap bag will be discarded or covered by the better bag. That's the end of the cheap bag's advertising career.

4. Hasty generalization is one of the major problems of personal experience. We generalize from one or two instances that happened to us or that is in our own personal observation. What is more believable than actual, first-hand experience? Our meal at the dinner buffet was mediocre, so that buffet is not very good. We've seen two instances of a high efficiency toilet breaking down (and in the last month, too!), so those toilets must be prone to breaking.

5. The resolution on many televisions has gotten so high now that the makeup on the models is clearly visible, rendering them less attractive.

6. Why don't these companies use aging, bald fat men to advertise their products instead of voluptuous young women?

7. Wicked Audio. More than just a brand name that exploits rebellion, it is a cultural marker of the shift away from an interest in righteousness toward an interest in its opposite. To use words designating evil as a brand name or to describe something held up as valuable by using negative words not only appeals to the prideful heart, but encourages the confusion about what is truly good.

8. When you lost a game of chance played at a booth to try to win a product, does that diminish your interest in buying that product or any product from that company? "You're a loser. Now buy something from us. Loser."

9. Several ads showed the American family smiling together (because they own or use the product, no doubt): A husband and wife (in their early thirties I'd say), a son (maybe 7 or 8), a daughter (maybe 6 or 7). All Caucasian. Son always a bit older than the daughter. Is that stereotyping? Is the dream American family a stereotype?

10. What good does it do to arm them with technology and cyber skills but to fail to teach them values and discernment?

11. You want to tell them, "The sound from your tiny speakers stinks," but all you say is, "Interesting" or "Nice."

12. You want to tell them, "The sound from your tiny speakers stinks, and the music you choose to demo the speakers makes them impossible to evaluate, since the music itself stinks even on good speakers.

1843. As I mentioned in an earlier Glimmering, schizophrenics are very logical. They can engage with you in a long series of logical explanations for their bizarre behavior:

"Why do you put patches of aluminum foil on the windows and under the bed?"

"To short out the zapper beams FBI is shooting at me."

"Why is the FBI shooting electric bolts at you?"

"They're trying to kill me so I won't reveal what I know."

"Why don't they want you to reveal what you know?"

"Because then everyone would know that the USA is really ruled by the Stromagite group."

This kind of logical explanation can go on indefinitely. The problem is that while logical, the schizophrenic is irrational. The claims are preposterous and false on the face. They don't stand up to reason.

It struck me just recently that evolutionary theory is just like this: logical but irrational. Evolutionists can describe things in logical order all day long (except for the circular reasoning involved in explaining natural selection and the survival of the fittest). But the theory is preposterous and does not stand up to reason. Just a look at the complexity of the interacting processes of every cell in every living thing makes it obvious that non-directed, random chance mutations as the mechanism of creation is a non-starter. It won't get evolution down the runway, much less allow it to fly. In fact, that explanation won't even open the hangar doors.

1844. Atheist. Noun. A person who hates God, often because of early problems with the person's natural father, and who attempts to punish or hurt God by encouraging other people to stop believing in God.

1845. Before you criticize or disagree with what you are reading or hearing, be sure you understand what you are reading or hearing.

1846. God's reasoning behind his plans for us is often opaque to us because it is God's reasoning, not ours. See Proverbs 20:24.

1847. In a normal person, the brain takes insane ideas (generated from brainstorming, for example) and makes them mutatis mutandis rational and practical. In a mentally ill person, the brain takes rational and practical ideas and makes them insane.

1848. To live for entertainment is to worship at the altar of the self. We should spend our time and energy advancing the kingdom of God or the course of civilization or at least the life of another human being. Are philosophy, wisdom, and spiritual truth so uninteresting that we cannot devote a few hours to such higher pursuits? Must we watch *another* movie, *another* reality show, *another* music video?

1849. James says, "You don't have because you don't ask" (James 4:2b). That's true in the worldly realm, too. So many things are available for the asking, but we either don't know about them or haven't thought to ask or have assumed they aren't available.

1850. Okay, now class, remember that evolution operates on the basis of directionless, random, chance mutations, most of which are harmful, but "selection pressure" results in natural selection through survival of the fittest. We can tell they are the fittest because they survive. And they survive because they are the fittest. Oh never mind. The point is, in theory, evolution is blind, deaf, and dumb and without purpose or direction. All you see around you is a glorious accident.

But this is how evolutionists talk: "The evolution of morality required a whole new set of decision-making machinery. The mind needed to evolve some structure that would keep it from hurting other people." And, "We are designed to feel one another's pain. . . . Sympathy is one of humanity's most basic instincts, which is why evolution lavished so much attention on mirror neurons. . . ." And, "Evolution has programmed us to care about one another." (These from Jonah Lehrer, *How We Decide*, pp. 175, 194, 195.) Wait a minute: *evolution required, needed to evolve, lavished attention, programmed us,* and — *we are designed???* Wow, this evolution person certainly seems to have god-like powers.

1851. Thinking of instruction manuals, Darxul read from the *Book of 100 Lies*:
    34. Installation is easy.
    35. No tools required.

1852. Why is it that installation instructions so often show tools you cannot use in the actual installation? Use a crescent wrench to tighten a center nut up under a sink? I don't think so.

1853. The happiness we get through achievement is known as self-esteem.

1854. **Dialog.**
    "Why is it that goodness, righteousness, truth, virtue — all are always in the minority, struggling to win adherents against a cultural tide flowing the opposite way?"
    "Because people love darkness more than they love light."
    "Yes, but why?"
    "Because their deeds are evil."
    "Yes, but why?"
    "Because they think their evil deeds are the way to happiness."
    "No, I don't believe that."
    "People wouldn't sin if it weren't fun."

"I'm not so sure about that. Evil is an ideology, and ideologues pursue their ends by means that cause them—and everyone else—pain and suffering."

"Are you saying that people do evil things for the sake of good? That evil people are misguided idealists?"

"Nope. Evil people are motivated by self-worship, which causes them to take on the role of rebel or control freak or cruel master. Anything to pump up their egos."

"So, evil people suffer from low self-esteem? I thought you said that pride was the problem with evil. Or is your conclusion that proud people have low self-esteem?"

1855. **Lessons from a Marriage, New Series, 1.**

1. When you and your spouse meet at the end of the workday, finding your spouse smiling and happy to see you is more powerfully comforting than you might believe if you haven't experienced it. To the not yet married and the married but unsmiling, then, take note and cheer yourself up by cheering your spouse up. For the dictum, "You will be just about as happy as your spouse," is fundamental. If you want to be happy, make your spouse happy.

2. When you leave the cap off the toothpaste or leave the coffee maker on when you leave for work, a good spouse is not the one who suppresses the upset feeling and the urge to comment. A good spouse is the one who simply isn't bothered by the situation in the first place. I mean, lighten up, folks.

1856. Concentrate on the happiness of others rather than your own happiness, and you'll get both.

1857. Every person has a limited capacity joy tank. Once it is full, you can't add more to it until it drains. Take your girlfriend to dinner at a restaurant she's always wanted to visit, then to an amusement park, then to a movie. Then give her a bouquet of flowers and a box of her favorite candy, then a gift card to her favorite store. Back at the amusement park, let's say she was joyous and happy and smiling. By the time you gave her the flowers, she was thanking you perfunctorily. Had you waited a few days for her joy tank to empty, she would have been ten times happier about the flowers than she was after her joy tank had reached its capacity on the amusement park day. So the point is to pace the pleasures and blessings (or gifts and treats, if you want a mundane expression), spread out over time.

1858. The Gadarene response (Luke 8:26-39): "Oh, we see that you can cure mental illness with a word and cast out a huge quantity of demons, so please leave." Yes, they would rather have crazy, violent people tormenting them than the presence of God. Sounds so contemporary.

1859. It used to be that only the young resented being given advice about life. Now everyone, it seems, is above instruction. Such an attitude stems either from pride or from postmodernism, which tells us that there are no facts, physical or moral, so that all admonitions about behavior are but mere opinions. And what could be more impudent than a situation where someone is attempting to regulate my behavior by his opinion?

1860. The most powerful learning, and the road to expertise, it is said, comes from studying your own mistakes. This fact does not bode well for modern society, since our culture tells us that all misadventures are someone else's fault. In other words, we don't make mistakes; other people make mistakes. So, what is there to learn?

1861. Why is English such a difficult language to learn? "Tom was fixing the joint in a drawer when his joint started to hurt. He went down to a joint for a drink, where he ended up smoking a joint with a stranger. The authorities from a joint taskforce suddenly entered. Tom was arrested and ended up in the joint."

[July 21, 2013; age 62]

1862. With amplification, a two or three man band can make as much noise as a 110 piece orchestra. And sound is not the only thing that can be amplified. A message can be amplified too. And everyone has a message he wants to be shouted from the housetops. That's why so many people study concepts such as going viral, meme theory, "contagious" sharing, and so forth. (Um, and not to mention self-publishing.)

1863. Once more with attention and thoughtfulness: The best things in life are free. Think—love, kindness, beauty, friendship, the enjoyment of nature, salvation, fresh mountain air and clean mountain water.

1864. If you can spend the time profitably while you are waiting, think how much wiser you can become. You could read something of value or you could just think. Thinking processes the experiences of life, and meaning is the result of thinking. How much time we waste waiting in line, or waiting for the doctor or the mechanic, or waiting for the show to start or for someone to get ready. And how do we spend that time? Playing with a smart phone, sending inane texts, talking with someone else about food or clothing.

1865. The question has arisen: Which is more important—love or truth? And why? Interestingly, nearly everyone I ask says love. When I tell them that truth is more important because without truth you cannot have love, nearly all of them assume that I'm claiming that love is not important. But love is of tremendous importance, and is among the best of things. And that is exactly why truth is more important. Without truth, "love" is only a delusion or a confidence game or both. And when the best of things is perverted, it becomes the worst of things.

1866. In small matters, truth is sacrificed to love. "Does this dress make me look fat?" Possible answers:

    A. No, donuts make you look fat, not the dress. [humorous true answer]

B. No, the dress doesn't make you look fat. You are fat. [straight truth]

C. Does this shirt make me look stupid? [evasive answer]

D. Why no, not at all. You look beautiful. [truth killed for the sake of love]

E. The dress makes you attractive. [escape from the horns of a dilemma by answering a different question.]

1867. Consider these:

"Sanctify us by your truth. Your word is truth."

"You shall know the truth and the truth shall make you free."

"Worship in spirit and in truth."

"I am the way, the truth, and the life."

Something tells me that truth is important to God.

1868. When Jesus calmed the wind and the waves, the disciples' jaws dropped. "What kind of a man is this, that even the wind and the sea obey him?" (Matthew 8:27). This reminds us that understanding often requires faith, and faith requires imagination — the ability to conceive something beyond our everyday experience.

1869. Darwin, Marx, and Freud — creators of three nineteenth century fantasies that still hold the imaginations of many. Three dreams from which so many refuse to awake and face the real world.

1870. How do people end up with so much expensive junk in their lives? Their loved ones give it to them as gifts. And you can't throw away an expensive gift from a loved one. I've overheard a woman in a store tell the clerk, "I want to get a really good fishing reel for my husband. What do you recommend?" She can pay a lot of money for a reel, but her husband might not like it. What's he to do?

1871. Online reviews. If a product has a bunch of five-star reviews and a bunch of one-star reviews, with some people extolling the virtues of it, while others are calling it worthless junk, saying it doesn't even work, does that reflect on the variations in the product (some good and some bad), or does it reveal the variations in the people who bought the product, with some being competent users and others not? Or does it reflect a propaganda war between the product's manufacturers (or marketers) and its competitors?

1872. When famous atheist philosopher Thomas Nagel rejects Neo Darwinism, is that a case of the Emperor's New Clothes being called out by a child? The materialists/naturalists are naked after all.

1873. The secret to success is to give people more than they expect. This secret works in business, marriage, teaching, friendship, politics. The problem is that when you consistently exceed expectations, the bar is raised, and expectations are higher. So an important part of success is the management of expectations. Manage expectations down and delivery up.

1874. Sometimes expectation management is difficult and exceeding expectations is impossible. Too many marriages run into difficulty because of a crisis in expectations. One spouse (or both) has a whole vision of what marriage and their spouse will be like, while the other spouse simply is not on that page—or even not reading the same chapter.

1875. Genius is good luck plus hard work. And a little bit of smarts. Or maybe enough smarts to recognize the good luck and where the hard work should be focused.

1876. The ideologues construct a plausible narrative and repeat it endlessly, even after it has been decisively disproved. This, by the way, is the very definition of propaganda. As time passes, the endless repetition reifies the narrative and truth is lost in a footnote.

1877. The question, "What makes any man attractive?" is usually answered with, "Wealth." Or at least the saying, "Wealth looks good on any man," seems to imply that, tall or short, fat or thin, handsome or ugly, being rich can make a man appealing to women.

The next question is, "What about women?" Or in formal terms, "What makes any woman attractive?" My answer is, "Happiness." When a man, young or old, meets a woman, young or old, he prefers a happy one. Women with baggage, resentments, depression, cynicism, bitterness, anger and the like are just not appealing because men perceive them as more trouble than benefit.

In romance, while women tend to focus on what they can get out of a relationship (which, of course is not good — it's just reality), men usually produce a cost-benefit calculation to see how much effort and trouble the relationship will require, and, compared to the expected benefit, whether the relationship is worth it. A happy, agreeable, companionable, friendly woman has enormous appeal. The desired traits might be summed up by "amiability."

There's a famous saying, "Men marry because they are tired; women, because they are curious. Both are disappointed."

1878. "With the fruit of a man's keyboard he will be satisfied; he will be satisfied with the product of his fingers." — Proverbs 18:20, Doax version.

1879. After a while, one finds the constant pandering of the entertainment media quite irritating. Movies and pop songs are all about the sluttification of American girlhood. From Disney's Aladdin, "There's no one to tell us no," to American Girl's "I don't listen to Mommy," the throwing off of moral restraint is everywhere.

1880. The world measures success by how far the boat sailed. God measures success by how big a wake the boat left. It's not the distance we cover or the people we meet that counts, but the impact we have on those we meet and the ripples that spread out from our passing.

1881. About men wanting happy women. The attractive woman is happy, cheerful, companionable, easy going—and vulnerable. Men have protective instincts that blossom when a woman shows vulnerability.

1882. Some people can connect the dots and know what's going on. Others can connect some of the dots and have at least a partial view. A few can see the dots but don't see their relationship. And then there are those who just can't see the dots at all. But they are not the most to be pitied. Real pity remains for those who cannot even imagine that the dots exist.

[September 26, 2013; age 62]

1883. Why are people not happy? Because they think life is about them. If you think life is about you, you can't be happy because life can never be enough about you. The way to be happy is to serve others—to give yourself away, as I have put it somewhere else. Wives are called to serve their husbands because women are more emotional than men. Women think about their feelings more and dissect whether they are happy and fulfilled. Men just go through life by going through life.

1884. "You will find that all the world preaches to an attentive mind; and that if you have but ears to hear, almost everything you meet teaches you some lesson of wisdom" (William Law, *A Serious Call to a Devout and Holy Life*, Chapter 13). If you want to grow, you have to look around.

1885. "Remember that there is but one man in the world, with whom you are to have perpetual contention, and be always striving to exceed him, and that is yourself" (William Law, *Serious Call*, Chapter 18). Strive always for your new personal best.

1886. **Free.** adj. 1. included in the price of something else. 2. paid for by someone else. 3. just pay processing, handling, packing, and shipping charges, plus tax. 4. at no cost until you become addicted. 5. without monetary costs, only costs to character, integrity, morals, and the like. 6. provided to you courtesy of the American taxpayer. 7. paid for by government money printing presses.

1887. It used to be said that biological evolution proceeded by one undirected, chance mutation at a time, happening many times over many years. But now that we know the complexities of the cell, the mechanisms of the Venus fly trap, and the process of metamorphosis, the Neo-Darwinian synthetic theory — one mutation at a time, undirected, et cetera, is clearly a non starter. What evolutionists are forced to believe now is a massively parallel, synchronous, symbiotic, undirected, upward directional, uncompromised-by-harmful mutations change.

1888. The perception of complexity and ambiguity is taken as a sign of superior analysis, just as writing in an obscure or even opaque style is taken as a sign of sophistication.

1889. "I'm not happy."
"Honey, you need to think of yourself more."
And so it starts. The advice that to be happy you should be more selfish. The problem is that a truly happy person — who actually knows how to be happy — would never give that advice. Happy people know that the secret to personal happiness is to serve others — to think of others' needs rather than your own wants: to give yourself away, so to speak.
If someone tells you to think of yourself first, look at that person closely and you'll find an unhappy person who can't learn to serve. Selfishness just doesn't work.

1890. A lot of pop tart entertainment has left mere music behind. The lyrics now are either mind-numbingly repetitive or unintelligible—because they simply don't matter. The music is mostly a percussive rhythm with an optional melody buried underneath.

The exhibition of pop tart presentations is no longer a concert. It's a performance, and not necessarily a musical performance. The star wears a dress made out of meat, or a see-through costume, or swings nude on a wrecking ball. None of this advances music. It is done to advance the performer. Done for shock value. Why else would we see a music video where the performers dance around singing while poisoning a restaurant full of people and a dog?

We are in the "attention economy" now, and to get and hold attention amid all the competition, too much of the culture has chosen to crank up the stunt ratchet and go for ever more outrageous spectacle.

1891. Too many people are interested only in proving who or what they are *not* rather than who or what they *are*. The question to ask any rebel is, "Just what are you *for*?" (And maybe, "What are your plans for building it?")

1892. We grow impatient with whatever or whoever we view as a means to an end—a job, a person, a college education. Since they are not our real goal, we are anxious to get past them as quickly as possible. So we treat them as an almost expendable irritant. The key to enjoying these things, then, is to treat them as worthy ends in themselves, as things or people to be relished and enjoyed.

1893. Sometimes God teaches us by negative example when we would have ignored the positive example. If we were given timely blessings, we might have ignored or not attended to them, or not valued them appropriately. But by getting them late, we learn their value (having had to live without them for a while) and we learn the value of timeliness: he who gives quickly gives twice. Let us not procrastinate in doing good.

1894. One of the less recognized consequences of information overload or data glut is the trivialization of truth. There is such a constant inflow of new information, added to the already huge quantum now in existence, that people are growing less and less serious about—less and less seriously committed to—the truth claims or implications of any of it. "You claim that X is true? I've heard the opposite claim, together with sixteen variants, twelve alternatives, and fourteen intermixtures." Or, "Sure, I believe that, I guess. It's just one truth among a million others that I believe."

1895. A brief comment about God:
Remember the attention and the intention of God. God pays attention to everything that goes on in his creation and it's his intention to respond. He is serious about sin.

1896. Just one more sign that the world has gone crazy is that our ever more complex, information-drenched world has responded to too much data smog not by creating elegant simplification techniques, but by embracing thought habits and information processing practices that only make things worse. It's the practice of anti-everything.

Anti-simplicity. Oh, you simply cannot simplify this concept, process, or interpretation. People who simplify are called simplistic. When some egohead tells someone at the party, "I couldn't explain it in terms you would understand," that's anti-simplicity.

Anti-intelligible. And, of course, the complex concept must be described using an abstract jargon with five nouns modifying a sixth. "The object analysis instrument report metric channel displays bifurcated anomaly data when a system interrupt obtains."

Anti-affirmative. To affirm something or concur with someone is now interpreted as the result of shallow thinking and superficial analysis. It's the person who finds a flaw (brilliant observation) or error (how astute of you) who gets the praise and esteem of colleagues, because it is interpreted as deep, careful thinking.

Anti-generalization. Instead of attempting to harness some little speck of the quantum of knowledge by generalizing or categorizing it, we are told to avoid "totalizing narratives," and stick with anecdotal arguments. No collected statistics, please.

Anti-rational. Reason works with categories and, indeed, with generalizations. So it must be oppressive and hence exiled.

1897. Lessons Learned from Attending DevLearn13 in Las Vegas

1. The power of habit? Love of the familiar? Fussy for one's own preference? Every morning, the conference offered endless, free, fresh, hot, tasty coffee (with real half and half), yet more than 100 people lined up at a nearby Starbuck's to buy their morning jolt.

2. Presenters, even some with slide shows, don't present quite what was scheduled when they would rather discuss something else, something closer to their hearts. "Here's a captive audience; now I can unload on them." The tolerable are those who have a pet hobby they want to let their hearers in on. The worst are those who want to talk about themselves.

3. We too often think about what we lack instead of what we have. Thus our complaints exceed our gratitude. We should thank more than we ask.

Remember when you pray this is your task:
That you should always thank more than you ask.

4. It's interesting how faddish people are in so many areas: clothes, games, cars, and technology. Even in information systems. I happened to mention MOOCs (Massive Open Online Courses), which have just recently become all the rage, when a presenter at the conference said, "Oh, MOOCs are going away." In another session, I mentioned how we used QR codes on posters to extend learning, and someone said, "Does anyone still use

QR codes?" There seems to be an ego pump to be not only on the leading edge into a new technofad, but also on the leading edge out—to declare that you are so hip that you have already left behind what is still in play among the less advanced.

1898. On modern (or is it postmodern) seekers:

> *They eagerly pursue whatever's new,*
> *And have no thought nor care for what is true.*

1899. Anger is a choice, as demonstrated by those who turn it off to speak to a stranger on the phone, and then turn it on again to continue assaulting their object of wrath.

1900. Riddle: What do people have in great abundance but are extremely stingy in sharing with those in need?

Answer: "Please," "Thank you," and "I'm sorry."

Comment: All of us have an infinite supply of these powerful, uplifting, and healing words, but we are miserly in giving any of them away. Maybe if someone saved our life, we might afford a brief, "Thanks."

1901. Wearily, Darxul looked upon the foolish, the thoughtless, and the ignorant, and attempted to help them ward off destruction by reading to them from the *Book of One Hundred Lies:*

36. If we don't pass this new law, sick children will die.

37. This is completely safe.

38. This new government program will save taxpayers money.

39. All I'm interested in is what is fair.

40. That fine print is just standard contract language.

1902. Understanding is Power (Proverbs 8:14). Knowing God brings understanding (Proverbs 9:10). Therefore, power comes from knowing God.

[November 9, 2013; age 63]

1903. **Ideas from reading** *How Could You Do That?* **by Laura Schlessinger.**

1. "We all need something to grab on to when we conceive of letting go of the familiar" (32). Certainly true in the world of ideas and theories. An old theory won't be abandoned until a new theory is available to take its place. (Thomas Kuhn makes this point in *The Structure of Scientific Revolutions*). In relationships, people sometimes haven't identified the new person or situation to go to before they abandon the old, so they rush thoughtlessly into some not-so-great opportunity or into the arms of the first person who shows an interest—who is often a predator, abuser, or plain vanilla jerk.

2. "We are what we do" (35). Better, "We become what we do." As Aristotle remarks somewhere, "Action leads to belief." When you do something over and over and it becomes a habit, it also defines you.

3. "What you choose to do under difficult conditions speaks to who you are and what you are like, more than what you do in so-called normal times" (54). People who make bad choices sometimes try to deny that they chose what they did freely. But very few circumstances make us choose badly.

4. "It is not the greatness of how life is going that makes an individual happy, it is attitude" (57). And people can choose their attitude. So many unhappy marriages could be happy if only spouses would understand this.

1904. We sometimes pretend that we don't have a choice, in order to defend a choice that we know is a poor one.

1905. **What makes evil, sin, and Satan so attractive?**

1. Rule breaking. People love the feeling of throwing off constraints, feeling free, no boundaries, no rules. Actually they like the presence of rules so that they can break them. If God had not told Adam and Even not to eat from the Tree of Knowledge of Good and Evil, they probably wouldn't have

gone right over to it when Satan suggested a snack. Nothing makes a thing more desirable than prohibiting it.

2. Energy. Doing wrong often involves doing so energetically, and energy is connected to excitement. The thrill of "putting the pedal to the metal" (that is, floorboarding it) and speeding down the road of error, is irresistible.

3. Surprise. The unexpected appeals to us, sometimes because it appears to be something new, and we confuse novelty with creativity; and sometimes the unexpected makes us fearful, and we confuse fear with power. And power is entrancing, seductive, a magnet to the soul in the same way a candle flame draws a moth.

1906. Making good choices is so important because you can damage the rest of your life in five minutes — or less — with a bad choice.

1907. Every choice is made in the context of our personal set of values, our moral set. Sometimes we choose something we know is wrong, but it is to be hoped that our values are strong enough to influence — to determine — the right choices.

1908. Happiness is not a goal. It is a byproduct. The purpose of life is not to be happy. The purpose of life is to serve God. Serving God comes through serving others: to be useful, loyal, responsible, compassionate. And to be these things when it is difficult to do so. Do this and you will find happiness. Or rather, happiness will find you.

1909. When you die, will your grave stone say, "He consumed a lot of products," or "He made a positive difference to others"?

1910. "I feel like my life doesn't matter."

"Well, what have you done to make it matter?"

"What do you mean?"

"You make your life matter — to others — by contributing to the ease and happiness of their lives."

"But I'm talking about me."

"Yes, and that's your problem. Stop thinking about yourself, become a servant, a helper, a solution for others, and, amazingly enough, you'll find that your life matters and that you can feel good about yourself."

1911. What you do reveals who you are. Actions are built from the blueprint of your character. You do what you are. Beliefs (values) lead to actions.

1912. Who you are is determined by what you do. Actions lead to beliefs. Thoughtless indulgence, compromise, and selfishness transmogrify into firm beliefs. Can we call them "values," or "anti-values"?

1913. If you forgive a wrong by your spouse, you must never bring it up again. If you bring up an old wrong during an argument, you have never really forgiven it. Therefore, you must (1) apologize for lying about having forgiven it, (2) apologize for being a hypocrite all this time, and (3) apologize for introducing a red herring into the argument instead of remaining focused on the current issue.

1914. Advice I read somewhere: If you are having difficulty in your relationship, imagine that it's now six months later and that your relationship is nearly perfect. What is one thing you can do today that will put you on the path to that future state six months from now?

1915. Dr. Laura Schlessinger's *as if* advice: If your feelings for your spouse have turned hostile, act *as if* they were still warm and loving. (This reminds me of Aristotle's idea that action leads to belief.) Yes, act happy. Act friendly. Act loving. Act warm. Act agreeable. You'll be surprised.

1916. Plan for your plans to change.

1917. Your quality of life does not consist in how many things you own but in how many people you serve.

1918. Wanting something is often a temporary idle lust. If you wait awhile before you buy that impulse item, chances are you won't want it anymore.

1919. Men need women. Men feel awkward letting that need show. And men want to feel needed by women. But they don't know how to let women know this.

1920. We are impatient because our souls are immortal but our bodies live in a transitory world.

[January 6, 2014; age 63]

1921. One person's fact is another person's transparent superstition. Ideologues are all about facts, but their facts are often slapped in the face by reality, who prefers that facts actually match what's true and real.

1922. Yes, there are more facts than ever. But that doesn't mean we are any closer to truth and beauty. What it does mean is that we need to engage all the more carefully in that great work of life, interpretation. (Yes, one of my very favorite proverbs is, "The central work of life is interpretation.") When a fact struts up to us, claiming to revolutionize our worldview, rather than bow down to it, we need to ask, "Is this really a fact? Is there any truth content? How much?" A fact with ten percent truth in it doesn't impress one much. And after we get past the questions of slant, distortion, partiality, and deception, we still need to hold it down with one hand and use our drill driver with the other hand to drive some three-inch drywall screws through the attachment holes and into the fact to put a handle on it. Only then can we pick it up, turn it around, and ask, "What, if anything, does this mean?"

1923. A good cook watches what the customers eat. A great chef watches what the customers don't eat.

1924. Before you kick the supporting beams of Western Civilization out from under your feet, make sure there isn't a noose around your neck.

1925. "In the beginning was Reason, and Reason was with God, and Reason was God. Reason was in the beginning with God. All things came into being through Reason, and apart from Reason nothing came into being that has come into being. In Reason was life, and the life was the light of men." —John 1:1-4 (Doax version)

1926. Why do we think that "free" means that no one had to pay for it? "Free" means that someone else paid for it, and that someone is often us. In that case, "free" means "you already paid for this," or "that is included in the price." "Buy this car and get free oil changes for a year," or "Buy this boat for $10,000 and get a trailer free." Might as well just say "included," but "free" is such a magic word.

In other cases, "free" means "paid for by someone else." "Free sample," "Free brochure, take one," and so on means that the marketer paid for the item for you. Similarly, salvation is free in this latter sense. Jesus paid for it on our behalf.

I suppose that quibblers could argue that a sign on a vacant lot saying, "Free dirt," would be a case of something absolutely free, since the lot's owner wants to get rid of the dirt. We can grant that, and even decline to offer the counter quibble that hauling the dirt away will incur some cost.

1927. There is a price or consequence for everything—and we hate that fact. This is why the entertainment industry spends so much effort to create products that display pleasure, rule breaking, even cruelty, all without consequences. We want our fantasies about self-indulgence without responsibility to come true.

A derivative of this is the plot where the hero must oppose the authorities and break all kinds of laws and regulations in order to save the world, either from terrorists or from the authorities themselves.

In this latter case, where the authorities are the villains, the entertainment folks show their conflation of and confusion between authority and authoritarianism. One wonders if equating these concepts is intentional, given the hatred for authority of any kind that's so often a theme of our cultural influencers.

1928. Work is the engine on the railway of dreams.

1929. When you hold a grudge against someone for hurting you, you perpetuate the hurt—you hurt yourself again every time you remember the original hurt.

1930. Anger accelerates the mouth and decelerates the brain.

1931. You can't win an argument with a six-year-old, especially when that six-year-old has lived for twenty-five years.

1932. The fact is, many people have an innate desire to punish others, and an enjoyment in doing so. Think about the driver who gives you a long blast of his horn after you almost blocked his way or slowed him down. He knows his horn is humiliating and that a good blast will make you feel hurt. But you both know that the blast won't do any real good. You cannot really repent for what was basically an accident, and the honker's driving is not going to be lessened because of the honking. The only reason for the honk was to punish you and to give the honker a feeling of superiority and righteousness.

In a nutshell, we have cruelty fed by pride. Yes, there it is again, pride, causing so much of the misery in the universe. Now it's up to stimulating the gigantic self-esteem into a proud punisher. A punisher who enjoys causing humiliation.

1933. Faith is trust in someone or something before actual knowledge, extrapolated from past experience. It's like forecasting, where conclusions are based on known initial facts.

1934. The currency of progress in this world is ideas—because ideas are the source of choices. New idea, new choices; good ideas, good choices; bad ideas, bad choices.

1935. New ideas are the fertilizer of thought. New ideas are the parents of other ideas.

1936. They are poseurs, dogmatists, and ideologues—but they are sincere. Sincere, not about the ideas they seem to be selling with such passion and irrationality, but sincere in their commitment to be free and autonomous by rejecting and tearing down all structure and constraint.

1937. "The magic continues." The word *magic* sometimes means, "We don't know how it's done." Sometimes it means, "It's so surprising and unusual that it transports us emotionally." Sometimes, "It happens too fast for ordinary life rules to explain it." Magic therefore is a fast surprise.

1938. From Gutenberg through the 18th or maybe 19th century, most of the books read were religious books and much of the focus of life was on spiritual matters. But then enter the modern scholar. His focus, his selection of books, and his writing and teaching are all about the secular items from those ages. He wants us to believe that his narrow selection and focus was the reality of those times. In other words, the ordinary people of the world were always like our modern ordinary people.

A simple example: we read the salacious plays of Restoration drama rather than the religious books of the time.

1939. Have you ever met an a knee-jerk opposer, an automatic disagreer? Some poor folks are married to one of them. Imagine their lives:

"I just read an article saying that some spouses contradict or disagree with everything their partner says."

"Oh, I don't agree with that. I know lots of couples who always agree with each other."

"Well, you disagree with everything I say."

"No, I don't."

"Well, let's change the subject. Nice day, isn't it?"

"Actually it's too cold to be considered a nice day."

Of course, when it is pointed out that the spouse has once again contradicted the partner, there's always the unarguable comeback, "Can't I express my opinion?"

1940. Exaggeration is now the entry level of description. Call something adequate and it will be taken as an insult.

1941. New ideas are fragile and need nourishment and encouragement from others. They are like butterflies, flitting uncertainly and being pushed around in the wind.

1942. Hypocrisy is a betrayal of trust amplified by arrogance.

1943. Modern movies and television and Internet video are all mostly visual landfill.

1944. Everyone submits to one authority or another. The claim of so-called rebels that they want to throw off all authority is either a lie or a self-delusion. What they want is to throw of some particular authority — social mores, law, Christianity, any restraint they don't like — so that they can submit to some other authority, and impose it on everyone else. Whether it's the authority of evolutionism, scientism, materialism, socialism, communism or just totalitarian hooliganism, all want and do submit to authority. The Russian revolution got rid of the Tsar, and implemented the authority of communism.

1945. Movies, popular songs, what is called poetry, legislation, the appeals courts — all are helping to implement the New

Grand Scheme: freedom from No. We don't want to be told No for something we want to do, eat, see, or experience, so we demand that our societal machines work toward that end.

And we don't want only permission to be free from No, we really want approval to reject No.

1946. Faith is the foundation of knowledge, the prerequisite to reason, and the necessary requirement for understanding. Knowledge rests on assumptions about the mind, the external world, cause and effect, and so forth, all of which must be accepted by faith. Reason, too, rests on assumptions about the reliability of the mind to proceed logically, that the world is coherent, that time is real, and so forth.

1947. Some people nourish hurts over a long period and refuse to forgive the wrongdoer. But why? Each time the hurt story is replayed in the hurt person's mind, it hurts again. The hurt is renewed and refreshed. The person who did the hurting is oblivious. The hurt story is just a way for the victim to continue self-hurting.

What benefit does the hurt person gain by nursing a grudge and by replaying the hurt story over and over?

What would the hurt person give up or lose if he or she stopped playing the hurt story and, in fact, forgave the person who did the hurting?

Does the hurt person expect to continue re-hurting himself by replaying the hurt story every time he thinks of or is reminded of the incident or behavior?

Is the hurt person waiting to forgive the hurter until the hurter suffers or is punished? So the hurt person will continue to replay the hurt story and be re-hurt indefinitely until the hurter repents? This is helpful to the hurt person? And what if the hurter is now dead?

Forgive the person who hurt you for your own sake and stop playing the hurt story.

1948. People have a thousand ways of displaying their pretentions to sophistication. Suppose you suggest eating at a certain restaurant and your team goes. When you all get back, the members of your team tell others about the experience thusly:

"We decided to throw caution to the wind and eat at a little hole-in-the-wall place."

"Yes, it was an unpretentious little eatery, but the food was okay for that kind of place."

"Yeah, strip mall cuisine isn't the best, but it takes the hunger away."

1949. "The most powerful computer in the world would require a billion years to crack this encryption."

"Of course, that implies that the software that actually created the encryption is working according to theory."

"And that there are no back doors, administrative passwords, or other weak entrances."

"In fact, the encryption is no stronger than the password or private key, which might be obtained through social engineering, hacking, or even simple theft."

1950. Irony involves the surprising reversal of expectation. It can be in the form of a sarcastic remark, where what is said is the opposite of what is meant:

[Fred slips on the ice and throws his books and papers everywhere before falling into the fountain] Tom: "Wow, Fred, great recovery from that little slip."

Or, irony can expose an incongruity between what we would expect and what occurs. Many jokes do this:

"Oh, my, the food here is just terrible."

"Yes, and the portions are so small."

. . . .

"Which one of those gentlemen is my surgeon?"

"The one holding the hammer."

1951. Three reasons that people get into arguments over leaving the cap off the toothpaste or not turning off the coffeepot:

1. A power struggle for control, both wanting to assert their rights and to demand that they are right: "My way or the highway."

2. A proxy for other problems.

3. Underlying hurt and need for validation, attention, affection. They are acting out because they feel they don't matter.

Informing all of these to some degree is the runaway ego of self-centeredness.

1952. God stays up all night waiting for your call.

1953. The butterfly and the shotgun. New ideas are fragile and tentative, requiring time to flesh out, just as the newly emerged butterfly must pump its wings with fluid before it can fly. And on first flight, the butterfly hopes to meet a friend with open palm where it can alight and where the friend can comment on its beautiful design and give it encouragement to fly higher. Too often, unfortunately, the friend has a shotgun and sees every butterfly as a target.

1954. Too many people now see boundaries only as restraints — as one big No after another. But boundaries are also protections. Would you like to get rid of the boundary markers for the land your house sits on? Or the lane boundary markers on the freeway? How much fun would tennis or football or baseball be without boundaries? And moral boundaries are not so different. Most people feel more secure and protected if their spouse observes the boundaries against infidelity. And aren't we protected more by boundaries against forgery, theft, fraud, and the like than if all those were just "caveat emptor" situations?

1955. Today's college students seem to lack intellectual courage. They take one look at a book and, if they cannot understand everything completely within two seconds, decide that it's too hard and put it down. "I don't know what *epistemology* means," they say. (One is tempted to retort, "Well, can you learn?" or "Why don't you look it up?" or "You might note that the book defines the term for you.") It's in the struggle to understand challenging material that our brains — no, we ourselves — grow and improve.

Ditto with the complaint that some books are boring. Oh, I have read a shelf full of boring books in my career. Fortunately, a few of them were important and had worthy knowledge, in spite of their authors' inability to write coherently.

1956. Unexpected consequences, or failure to think down the road. They retrofitted the old building with low volume toilets to save water. "Only a quart or so per flush," they bragged. But they didn't realize that the slope of the sewer pipes had been based on the original, higher volume of water per flush to move the waste along. The result was that the sewer pipes clogged up.

1957. Unexpected consequences #2. They undersized the air ducts to save money, and they increased the fan speed to get the needed air volume flowing to each register. But they didn't realize that the higher fan speed created a lot of noise from the air flow and the rattling air ducts, diminishing the peace and quiet of the building.

1958. There's no such thing as an insignificant improvement.

1959. Did you ever notice that the only time you make an excess amount of noise is when you're trying to be quiet?

1960. We buy something new, hoping it's better than its replacement, but it turns out to be only different. However, with our ego at stake, we declare it better and keep it. Returning it to the store would be an admission of defeat or incompetence.

It occurs to me that this is a man thing. Women buy and return truckloads of clothes, shoes, towels, knick knacks, and so forth all the time, without feeling any compunction at all. Returning items doesn't affect their self-image in the slightest.

1961. How self-centered we all are. We use ourselves as the standard of measure: We say, "It's hot in here," or "It's cold in here," rather than, "I'm hot," or "I'm cold." We say, "That guy is driving too slow; why doesn't he get out of my way?" instead of, "That guy is driving more slowly than I am; I wish he would move from in front of me."

1962. **Lessons from a Psychiatric Care Home**

1. Nicotine as Therapy. The patients line up at designated times to receive a cigarette. Three staff members work the line: one to manage the lineup, and two to read each patient's name, open a baggie with the patient's pack of cigarettes in it, and light the cigarette for the patient. It is known that some mental patients will chain smoke if given the opportunity, with the assumption being that they are unconsciously trying to self-medicate — the nicotine having a calming effect.

2. Library. A small library contains what appear to be cast off donations to the facility. About a third are pulp novels, but also included are a few classic novels, some nonfiction books (*What Every Woman Should Know about Men*), and one or two more esoteric reference books. Planning and intent are not part of the collection.

3. Compassion. As much as we hear about these "human warehouses," the staff here shows compassion in the form of accommodation. Visitors are allowed to meet with a patient in a private room. A fearful man is allowed to sleep on the floor in a protected corner of the hall. A staff member graciously accepts some food from a patient that the patient didn't finish. (Rather than reject the gift, the staff member accepts it and will throw it away later.)

1963. "Occasionally rising from among the wrongheadedness, embarrassments, misconceptions, fallacies, and preposterousness," wrote the critic, "there can be found a few good ideas — all of which are quoted from other authors."

1964. "That the novel is banal, derivative, and poorly assembled from other Grade D hack writers doesn't bother me as much," wrote the critic, "as the convoluted and torturous prose, which only occasionally manages to struggle up from opacity into ambiguity. Perhaps this is not such a fault after all because the reader doesn't really care what the wooden and robotic characters are doing, and if the reader does, the plot is so predictable that deciphering the sentences is unnecessary anyway."

1965. He calls under the pretense of wanting to help with a software problem, but soon you realize that he is a salesman, pedaling some service for a monthly fee. But what irritates you is his tone of voice or attitude. He probably doesn't realize it, but his voice conveys a combination of arrogance and condescension, as if he is saying, "I know how to use the right words to put fear into this schlub's heart so that he will sign up and pay plenty." The superiority and confidence leak past his control. He is surprised when you tell him no.

1966. When you write a book, you are saying, "I expect you to take several hours out of your life and spend them listening to me." My philosophy is that a book should be packed with enough material—ideas, practical applications, insights, and so on (humor, too) that the readers will think the time well spent. After all, we have only a limited number of hours of life. Is this book worth what it costs in your life?

1967. And now for some advice for team members or collaborators. The first piece of advice is
Never edit a document by committee.
Example 1: I remember working on a PowerPoint slide during a teleconference committee meeting.
"We should put in the fact that this rule applies to [blank] as well as [blank]."
"We already have 200 words on the slide."
"Well, we need to say this."
"And that [blank] is a prerequisite for [blank]."

"No it isn't."

"[Blank] has always been a prerequisite for [blank]."

"No, take that sentence out. We don't require that."

"Yes, we do."

And so it went for an hour.

Example 2: In another case, the editing proceeded this way:

"So far we have, 'Inform the caller to mail the request to us.'"

"We should change 'inform' to 'tell.'"

"No, 'tell' sounds too authoritarian. It should be 'ask.'"

"But 'ask' implies that we don't have to have the request mailed to us. It's mandatory."

"So we should say, 'Ask the caller to send us the mandatory form by mail.'"

"'Mandatory' should be 'required.'"

"I think we should say something friendlier, such as, 'Tell the caller that we need to have the form mailed to us.'"

"Why don't we just tell the truth, and say, 'Tell the caller that the government requires that we get a completed form by mail'?"

"'Filled out' or 'completed'?"

"'Government' or 'federal law'?"

"Why not, 'We are legally required'?"

1968. Just when you thought that writing a memo by committee was as bad as it could get, you get a draft document with requests for editing. You can do that. But there is a problem. The same document is being sent to six other people, to make edits also.

Example 1: Round Robin Editing, where the document is sent in sequence to a list of people.

Original Version: "Please put all trash in trash cans."

Joe's Edits: "Put all litter into trash cans."

Jane's Edits: "It is important that you place all disposables, trash, and garbage into the designated trash cans which are supplied for the purpose. They are located on each street corner in the downtown area."

Tom's Edits: "Throw all garbage into the labeled trash cans on the street corners."

Sandy's Edits: "Please be a responsible, good citizen by throwing your trash into the litter containers on the street corners."

Jim's Edits: "Please use the trash cans for all trash."

Example 2: Shotgun Editing, where several people make edits simultaneously and version control goes out the window.

Original version: "Keep off the grass."

Joe's version: "Stay off the grass."

Jane's version: "Please do not walk on the lawn because the variety of the grass is very delicate and foot traffic will quickly wear dead spots into the area, requiring expensive resodding to those unsightly areas."

Tom's version: "Stay on paved walkways. Do not walk on the grass."

Sandy's version: "Thoughtful folks don't walk on the planted areas."

Jim's version: "Walking on the grass is prohibited and will be punished to the fullest extent of the law."

1969. How we feel about a concept influences how we define it.

1970. How a concept is defined for us influences how we feel about it.

1971. What is the goal or purpose of a book of literary criticism written by an academic? Is it to explain the meaning of a text, offer historical background or gloss some esoteric references for the benefit of the reader? Oh, come now. For canonical works, most of that has been done and done pretty well in the 1940s, 50s, and 60s. So then, is the purpose to explain modern texts? No. To develop new, clarifying approaches or theories about a work or its author? No so much.

As an undergraduate, I visited a professor in his office, where I noticed a brand new book with his name on it. Jokingly, I said, "Is this going to be a best seller soon?"

He looked at the book and said very seriously, "Oh, no. This is a book for libraries."

If you will compare a typical work of scholarship about any author, past or present, with a popularizing book or an older work of scholarship, you will see what the professor meant. Modern books of scholarship (in the humanities, at least) seem to have the following priorities:

1. To help the writer get tenure

2. To impress the writer's colleagues with his or her sophistication, erudition, and vocabulary

3. To provide bona fides that the author is a worthy member of the scholarly community

I think this explains why there is so much opacity, posturing, bombast, and downright unintelligibility in so much academic writing. I had for a short time thought that the postmodernists were the major culprits, but I see that they are writing in a hallowed tradition of obscurantism and pomposity.

Samuel Johnson, in *Rambler* No. 1, notes that writers indulge an "ostentatious and haughty display of themselves."

1972. There seems to be an agreement among the literati that some of their ideas are so profound and exalted that they cannot be explained in simple terms. Didn't we teach in English 101 that you should be able to paraphrase a writer's ideas as evidence that you understand them? And shouldn't a writer be able to paraphrase his or her own ideas?

1973. Those who criticize are thought to be more intelligent or sophisticated than those who praise. Samuel Johnson says, "Censure is willingly indulged, because it always implies some superiority; men please themselves with imagining that they have made a deeper search, or wider survey, than others, and detected faults and follies, which escape vulgar observation."
—Samuel Jonson, *Rambler* 2.

1974. Impatience is one of the homely daughters of Pride.

1975. They call under the pretense of taking a survey, and then ask you to buy, donate, or sign up for something. Or they call and say, "This is not a sales call," and then proceed to put the pressure on you to buy something.

This raises a question. I have now learned that these outfits (as my father would call them) are willing to lie to me to get my attention. And do they now really believe that I am going to trust them by giving them money? The pretense of the call is actually a sort of con scheme. Didn't we learn not to fall for con schemes?

1976. Darxul shook his head sadly, realizing that some people actually think there is something new under the sun. He pulled *The Book of One Hundred Lies* off the shelf, dusted it off, and read:

41. This is not a sales call.

42. I'm just calling to make sure you are enjoying all the features of your plan.

43. I have good news for you.

44. You won't get a better deal than this.

1977. If you asked someone randomly on the street, "Which area of learning is the one that champions free inquiry, chasing the truth wherever it may lead, free from bias or ideology?" most people would say either, "There isn't one," (clever cynics), or "Science." That's the answer most scientists would give, too. And yet it seems that science is becoming an area of learning where right answers are more important than truth.

There is a pressure to conform to currently accepted theory and those who want to question it are punished in various ways. I could be thinking of evolutionary dogma, of course, but let's leave that lying by the side of the road for now. I was instead thinking of global warming—or its new name, climate change—as the poster boy. "Settled science" seems to mean that once the majority of scientists (or the most vocal or the most powerful) decide on an issue, everyone must agree or face the consequences.

It is a sad journey to read the history of scientific ideas and how violently and stubbornly old ideas were maintained and the new ones opposed. It's a wonder we still don't believe in phlogiston.

1978. Lessons from the Consumer Electronics Show, 2014

1. Until you can shop around and compare prices, it's often difficult to know whether a new item is priced well. At the show we saw a pulse oximeter that connected to a smartphone, priced at about $100. The device seemed novel, useful, and so forth. A few weeks later, an article recommended pulse oximeters for use when exercising, so I went online to check them out. Standalone meters start at $18.

1979. The lie is in the asterisk.
- ABSOLUTELY FREE SAMPLE* *Just pay shipping and handling, and your credit card will be enrolled for the cost of automatic monthly supplies.
- No cost or obligation.* *If you don't like the product, you can cancel at any time. Otherwise, there is automatic renewal.
- Act now and we'll double your order absolutely free.* *Just pay additional shipping and handling, processing and mailing.
- FREE SHIPPING* *Just pay a handling fee of $4.95.

1980. "How can we understand God and his nature?"

"Well, what can you compare him to?"

"That's the point. Nothing can compare with God."

"But if we can't compare God to anything, then we can't know anything about him."

"Well, what we usually do is employ inadequate metaphors, or anthropomorphic imagery, as in the strong arm of the Lord, or God seated on his throne. And we use other imagery, such as God hiding us in the shadow of his wings."

1981. Any attempt to describe God is an attempt to adumbrate the ineffable. It cannot be done very well, but it must be done.

1982. Advice for those who want to get revenge on past hurts from parents by punishing their spouses: Don't pay it back forward.

1983. What's missing from the lives of many people today is context, a view of how they fit into the big picture. Not so many years ago, people thought about the universe and what part they played in the "grand scheme of things." Today, people are concerned only with the universe of the self. As the focus of our lives and attention grows ever narrower until the scope of life is only as far as we can see into ourselves, we're losing connections.

1984. Knowing where we come from is important for many reasons, not the least of which is that such knowledge tells us where we are going. If you know the highway you're on, you have a much better chance of knowing where you're going than if you think you're going in a random direction.

1985. The emotional tone (attitude or mood) developed during one experience tends strongly to carry over into the next time period and is directed toward the next person met because emotions are so strong that they persist long after the experience that generated them.

- I was next to visit a nurse practitioner once, who had been propositioned by the patient before me. When I told her I wasn't sleeping well, she rather viciously demanded, "Why not?" Of course, that was the question I had hoped to have answered by her.
- I was treated with bubbly smiles and joy by a cashier at a grocery store one day. I was just beginning to wonder what it was about me that was so joy inspiring when I

learned that the girl had just talked to her boyfriend, who had apparently proposed.

The odd thing is not the fact that people can't control their emotions enough to reset their attitudes toward the next customer or person, but that the recipients of the emotional attitude, even when they know they are not the cause or intended subjects of the feelings, still are deeply affected by it.

1986. Regarding the power of emotions, discussed above. Many high school students are afraid to act in school plays because they will be pretending to be emotional. Not only do they not know how, but they are afraid they will get caught up in out-of-control feelings for a fellow actor.

There is some justification for this, as we witness how many professional actors and actresses begin affairs while on the set of a particular film.

1987. Reading supplies the raw material (ideas) for analogies, problem solving, creative thinking, understanding the world, and so forth. But "reading" used to mean perusing the text, thinking about it. saving favorite quotations, and if possible, sharing what one had learned with someone else.

But today, who has time for reading, thinking, and sharing? Haven't we abandoned quiet time (for reflecting, reading, writing, making and studying notes, testing ideas in real life) for the busyness of life? Got time on your hands? Tweet, text, fax, email, or phone someone so you won't have to spend the time alone with yourself. And, of course, that's the problem. We don't have time to think, so we do little thinking, and hence civilization advances more slowly than it ought.

As far back as 1750, Samuel Johnson, in his *Rambler* No. 2, noted that modern life has produced "a multitude fluctuating in pleasures, or immersed in business, without time for intellectual amusements. . . ." I guess that puts a crimp in my own hopes that this book will be a perennial best seller. Darn.

1988. A standard dictum of decision making is that people fear loss more than they hope for gain. This single fact explains a lot about human beings:

- We don't like risk. (Think of advertisers, "No risk!" appeal to cater to this.
- We want security and guarantees accompanying every decision. ("Satisfaction guaranteed!")
- We procrastinate and delay making decisions that would result in change and unknown results.
- We buy from those who emphasize the upside and who minimize the downside.
- Some people stay in toxic relationships because they are familiar and to leave would involve change and the unknown—risk and hope, which means a loss of security.

1989. One of the great inhibitors to learning, even greater than laziness or procrastination, is pride. Here are some of the ways pride gets in the way of learning.

- Proud people are afraid to ask questions because that would reveal their ignorance.
- Proud people laugh at others who don't know something the proud person does, thus hindering the learning of others. If you know you will be laughed at for asking a question, you likely won't ask it. ("Hah! You don't know what a thermal transducer is? How long have you been working here?")
- Proud people pretend to know already the subject under discussion, and sometimes make up or parrot ideas to prove it, thus introducing factual errors into the subject area.
- Proud people are often negative and critical, since, if they know little about the subject, they can always demonstrate both knowledge and sophistication about it by criticizing some aspect of it, thus showing superiority.
- Proud people often cement a particular viewpoint or set of "facts" into their heads and stubbornly hang on to

them, long after they have been shown to be false or in need of revision.

1990. One wonders what to do with a study that claims to have found that men and women speak the same number of words each day. That claim, as Samuel Johnson would say, "is overthrown by the experience of every hour." Perhaps there is some specific situation where the number is even, but in a freely open day, women speak substantially more words—what would you say? double, triple?—than men.

1991. Thursday.
    Me: "Hello. I'm Robert Harris. I'm trying to find out how to help [person] get help from [government program].
    Bureaucrat: "I can't talk to you without authorization from [person] to speak on his behalf."
    Me: "He can barely talk and can't fill out forms. How can I help him?"
    Bureaucrat: "I can send him the forms."
    Me: "Okay."

    Monday.
    Me: "We talked on Thursday about getting [person] help from [government program]."
    Bureaucrat: "No, we didn't. I would need authorization from [person] in order to talk to you about his case."

    Conclusion:
    If you try to discuss getting someone else help, but you are not an approved representative, you didn't really talk to the case worker. The case worker made no record of it, and so, in fact, *the call never happened.* You don't think anyone is going to get caught documenting an unauthorized call, do you?

1992. Isn't it interesting how, when there is only one source of information, we tend to credit it without skepticism? But when a second source arises that conflicts or has an alternative truth, we doubt both. Or at least our confidence in the first source is shaken.

Simple example: If we have a thermometer, thermostat, or temperature sensor, we believe what it says as long as the indication meets a face validity test. It's 95 degrees today? Sounds about right. But then a competing indicator says 90 degrees. Which is right? Or are both wrong? Do we average them together?

More unusual example: Who wrote the plays attributed to William Shakespeare? Well, duh. The guy from Stratford Upon Avon. But what about all that evidence for Francis Bacon or Edward de Vere or even Sir Henry Neville? Talk about shaking your assumptions. But then we face an impossible decision. (I know! Shakespeare's poems and plays were written by a committee!)

Remember those times you saw three or four appealing programs on at the same time, and your DVR was full or broken? Did you choose one or decide not to watch any of them?

1993. *The Nonexistent.* A book never written by a man who never lived. Oh, how we miss him.

1994. *The New Metamorphosis.* Where an insect turns into a man and is thought the worse for it. A satire. Of course.

1995. What makes an idea go from (1) an interesting philosophical commitment, which, if you argue against, you are asked to explain, to (2) a pet ideological commitment, which, if you argue against, you are asked to leave?

I remember well during my undergraduate years there were many professors who refused to take any kind of stand or express any conclusion or settled belief. Everything was tentative, relative, uncertain. Then, with the advent of postmodernism, everything became so multiplied, with infinite interpretations and innumerable beliefs, judgments, and so forth that making a commitment seemed foolish.

But now, we have politically correct litmus tests, where student and scholar alike must express approved opinions, work within the confines of "settled science," and make sure their conclusions harmonize with appropriate political dogma.

The lack of commitment and the requirement to support the "consensus belief" both free the professoriate from having to take the risk of saying something definite and thereby be criticized for being incorrect. It's part of the escape from personal responsibility that modern culture teaches and encourages.

1996. Let this Glimmering serve as a reminder to myself that I want to write a book about water. Water is the most amazing substance. It is useful as a solvent and thirst quencher, creates beauty through the plant and animal life it sustains, can be transmogrified (thanks Poe) to many other things. Ice, sleet, hail, steam, hydroelectric dams, snow (with no two snowflakes alike), filling lakes, oceans, streams, rivers. Drink it, bathe in it, wash the driveway with it, cook with it, and then wash the dishes with it, too.

1997. How long is it before we take a new blessing for granted? I'm just looking at a can of aerosol, foaming glass cleaner. Ought we not drop to our knees and thank God for such amazing and powerful tools? Why is it that we always just grab the tool — or the vegetables, or ice cream — and go on with our lives, not thinking about the depth and riches of meaning behind the supposedly simplest of tools.

Think how blessed we are with microwave ovens, prepared frozen food, dishwashers, hand tools of all kinds, grapes available in the winter, flown in from warmer climates.

1998. It's not what you look at but how you look. Your enjoyment of and meaning in life are not determined by the quantity of your observations or by any specific things you might choose to see. The quality of your life is due to the insights, the meanings gained from knowing how to look at things. With the proper thought, even ugly things can have beautiful meanings, if not some aspect of beauty in themselves.

1999. You don't have much time left on earth. Are you going to spend it gossiping, backbiting, criticizing, nagging, whining, complaining, being moody and cross, or are you going to make an effort to redeem what years may lie ahead? Think what a limited amount of time you have left — and get going.

2000. Mistake Number One is to use yourself as a standard to decide what others should be doing. Mistake Number Two is to use others as a standard to decide what you should be doing. Standards must be external, objective, not time bound, and insofar as possible, not culture bound, for culture-bound standards are often oppressive, unjust, and unstable. Just when you come close to becoming a cultural clone, the fad magazines all tell you you're outdated. And what creates more consternation than the accusation of following outdated morality?

2001. Decision making requires that seemingly impossible negotiation between analysis, deliberation, assessment, waiting for the envelope of opportunity to grow as large as is reasonable on the one hand, and on the other hand, the need to be decisive, to act in a timely manner, to make the decision with resolute confidence.

The Monday-morning quarterbacks are more than ready to drop the phrases, "paralysis by analysis," and "procrastination petrification" if you wait a moment longer than they deem appropriate. And, the same people or their friends will pronounce, "haste makes waste," "rush to judgment," and so on.

So many decisions have unusual or even unique features, and yet some people think there must be a book listing industry-standard decision-making timeframes.

2002. Some people make decisions about their personal behavior by asking the question, "Will this make me happy?" or even narrower, "Will this give me pleasure?" Others make such decisions by asking, "Will this make other people happy?" or perhaps, "Will this give other people pleasure?" And some are asking as well, "Will this give me peace of mind?" or better, "Will this leave my soul at peace?"

2003. The greatest piece of Greek wisdom was, "Know Thyself." But what does that mean? Check your driver's license to see who you are? No. It means that you should examine and understand your principles and the values that you operate by. What do you stand for? What do you believe in? To what or whom are you loyal? What is the most important thing in your life?

⌘⌘⌘

Concluding note.
If you enjoyed these Glimmerings, you might also enjoy my other books, *Glimmerings I*, *The Million Dollar Girl*, and *Seventy Stories and a Poem*.

And if you like the format of mostly short bites of food for thought, try some of these:

Marcus Aurelius, *Meditations*
Blaise Pascal, *Pensees*
Dag Hammarskjold, *Markings*
Georg Christoph Lichtenberg, *Aphorisms*
Baltasar Gracian, *The Art of Worldly Wisdom*

Colophon
Body text set in Book Antiqua 11-point type

www.ingramcontent.com/pod-product-compliance
Lightning Source LLC
Chambersburg PA
CBHW060920040426
42445CB00011B/715